James Rhodes

Fire on
All Sides

Quercus

First published in Great Britain in 2018 by Quercus Editions Ltd
This paperback edition published in 2018 by

Quercus Editions Ltd
Carmelite House
50 Victoria Embankment
London EC4Y 0DZ
An Hachette UK company

A CIP catalogue record for this book is available
from the British Library

PB ISBN 978 1 78648 245 7

10 9 8 7 6 5 4 3 2

Inside cover photograph © Denis Blais
Illustrations by Amber Anderson
Text designed and typeset by CC Book Production

Printed and bound in Great Britain by Clays Ltd, Elcograf S.p.A.

James Rhodes was born in London in 1975. A keen piano player, at eighteen he was offered a scholarship at the Guildhall School of Music and Drama, but went to Edinburgh University instead. James stopped playing the piano entirely and dropped out after a year. He ended up working in the City in London for five years. After a devastating mental breakdown that led him to be institutionalised, he took the piano up again. He is now a professional and applauded concert pianist, writer and television presenter. His memoir, *Instrumental*, which is currently being adapted for the big screen, became an international bestseller, as did his short book *How to Play the Piano*.

You can follow him on Twitter at @JRhodesPianist and visit him at www.jamesrhodes.tv

Praise for *Fire On All Sides*

'What [Rhodes] describes in *Fire On All Sides*, writing with the same passion and energy he has when talking, are less destructive, more life-enhancing avenues to cope with anxiety, depression and trauma that he has found effective . . . An earlier generation might have referred to Rhodes as a tortured genius and left it at that, but his life defies such casual, catch-all labels' *Daily Telegraph*

'*Fire On All Sides*, against the odds, is very funny . . . A highly readable book . . . With searing honesty, Rhodes lays the parts of himself out like the clothes he packs before a trip abroad' *Observer*

'Rhodes writes like he plays – with power and intensity . . . Deeply stirring' *Evening Standard*

'Brilliant . . . compelling . . . An important story that deserves to be told' *BBC Music Magazine*

'[Rhodes'] account of depression is achingly human' *Jewish Chronicle*

'The pages crackle with music's transformative power . . . A fitting companion to his first book, *Fire On All Sides* is indisputably bruising and unflinching, but it's also consoling to anyone who's felt like an outsider' *Sunday Business Post*

'There is no more passionate advocate for the power of music to heal a battered soul than James Rhodes' *Big Issue*

'James Rhodes has launched a small revolution' *El Mundo*

Praise for *Instrumental*

'Thrilling and harrowing . . . Unsurpassed and unsurpassable' *Sunday Times*

'There is an insight, often startling but always valuable, on almost every page . . . a tough, riveting read' *The Times*

'A mesmeric combination of vivid, keen, obsessive precision and raw, urgent energy' *Guardian*

'I don't think I've ever read an autobiography which is this exuberant, this full of life, this addictively readable' Mark Haddon

'A searingly honest, moving and compelling account of a life damaged by abuse but saved by music . . . This is a tough but beautiful book' Victoria Hislop

'A masterpiece of creative endurance . . . [Rhodes'] passion is his programme, his heart is his true instrument, and you might not read a more moral or more loving book this decade' Andrew O'Hagan

'Visceral and palpable . . . Among the most powerful pages I've read all year' *Scotsman*

'An extraordinary book . . . Rhodes proves that art and beauty do help; that life can be conquered day by day' *El Pais*

'A hand-grenade of a book' *Stern Magazin*

'An all-access pass to the sublime' *Los Angeles Review of Books*

For my son

THE JAMES RHODES TOUR

August–December 2016

Madrid · El Escorial · Canterbury ·

Bilbao · Hanover · Berlin · Dresden ·

Munich · Frankfurt · Mainz · Zürich ·

Hamburg · Vienna · Düsseldorf ·

Stuttgart · Bonn · Barcelona ·

Bristol · Cheltenham ·

Valencia · Zaragoza

Advisory Warnings and Listening Materials:

This book is not a memoir. Because I've already written one of those. This book is a journal that I kept while on tour. It's all here as I wrote it down at the time, rather than a more sanitised (sensible?), hindsight-friendly version.

A tour journal may sound as if it's going to be little more than a slightly dull, perhaps somewhat indulgent travel diary that I kept as I flew around the world exploring its most beautiful cities, playing the piano in stunning concert halls, discussing my creative process and eating incredible food. But bear with me.

Because yes, it's about those things – including the self-indulgent crap because it's me and I'm a narcissistic asshole – but it's more about the often searing pain and Herculean effort that goes with simply enduring and existing in this world for someone as ill-equipped in basic life skills as I am. As, to a greater or lesser extent, I believe we all are.

This book is about fantasy, fury, fucking and fire. Fire everywhere. In my brain, behind my eyes, in my chest.

Fire on all sides.

It's a book about music. About love. About hatred. About imperfection. Finally, maybe, it's a book about feeling OK with yourself.

For those of you who don't know me, I was physically abused when I was a kid. My PE teacher raped me from ages six to ten. If you fancy a little light reading, you can find out more in my memoir *Instrumental*. It describes the catastrophically chaotic aftermath of the effect of such abuse: drug addiction, psychotic breaks, suicide attempts and mental institutions. And it talks a lot about classical music, my reason for being. You'll find it in the comedy section.

While I'm hoping desperately that those of you who are still reading this haven't experienced child rape, I'm assuming the vast majority will have experienced trauma of some kind either directly or indirectly. Divorce, abuse, alcoholism, domestic violence, death, disease, poverty, *Love Island*. Take your pick; life is full of choices. And I'm also assuming that many, most, all of you know what depression and anxiety feel like. The sheer weight of those shackles, the quiet heroism of simply getting up, getting dressed and out of the house. How it makes day-to-day living excruciatingly difficult. The stress of having to behave the way people want you to behave because there are expectations, because showing your true self would be career or social suicide.

It's a game a lot of us play all the time – the game of making it look like everything is OK, that you know your shit and you're quite capable of adulting. As the singer Elliott Smith said before he killed himself, 'Everybody is [inconsistent]. Everybody pretends like they're more coherent so that other people can pretend that they understand them better. That's what you have to do. If everybody really acted like how they felt all the time, it would be total madness.'

I pretend a lot.

This book is not about *who* I am. It is about *how* I am. How, perhaps, we all are. The fact that I am a father, pianist, writer, ex-husband, Pisces, idiot is irrelevant. It is the how that is important. I'm convinced that *how* we endure and function in today's world is not only vastly more interesting than our job titles and bank balances and Instagram updates, but also something that brings us closer together at a time when so many things are pushing us apart. When the world in which we live seems to promise so much and yet deliver so little, admitting to our own imperfections and fragilities has the ability to unite us all in a way that is miraculous.

I've tried, with the best possible motives, to share with you all of the ugliness and rawness that's within me, because, even if I occasionally come across like an oversharer on a catastrophic first date, I think it's deeply important for us to see and be seen as we really, truly are. The nasty stuff is particularly evident when I'm touring, when travel, tiredness, pressure, stress, criticism and self-hatred are all amplified and come together in one horrible, sticky mess. I'm also starting from a very low point: still bruised from the consequences of a horrifying legal battle over the publication of my first book and in the process of divorcing. So there's a lot of introspection, insomnia and anger. Really quite a lot of anger because, well, there's a lot to be angry about.

For pretty much every second of every day for the last thirty-five-plus years my head has told me, in varied, imaginative and extravagant ways, that I'm no good. And that is what's at the heart of everything that is painful in my life: my mind and what it tells me.

And boy does it tell me stuff.

I have a thousand voices in there, an infinite amount of conjecture, projection, imagined slights, debates, discussions, fights. Oftentimes all at once. There is a breathtakingly fucked-up abuse of power here. My mind – my warped, broken, perspective-lacking, biased, out of control mind – has, for decades, been given carte blanche to dictate and regulate my entire outlook on life.

It turns out I am completely unequipped to define my own reality. Forget the normal, rational triggers that we all react to – hostility, criticism, rejection, heartache, pain. In my case, when my head isn't quite right, if someone *looks* at me funny, doesn't reply to an email fast enough, uses vaguely aggressive language in a text, unfollows me on Twitter, brings me the wrong food order in a restaurant, I want to kill or be killed. And I don't think I'm alone in this. Look around you – we are all, to a greater or lesser extent, splashing about in the same paddling pool of crazy.

I have a number of filters in my mind's eye that skew the entire world both inside and out. I see black when the rest of the world swears to me that it's pink. I can look at my life on paper and see that, rationally, it's exceptional. It is filled to the brim with love, prosperity, friendship, talent, opportunity, the expectation of good. And yet when I inhabit that life and witness it through my own head with its myriad filters, I am, frustratingly, in a self-built prison and can see no way out. Ninety per cent of my thoughts are designed to stop me from enjoying almost every aspect of my life and to keep me unhappy, unhealthy and unsettled. It's become excruciating.

Worst of all, although I know it's a lot to do with my past and the fact that I've had approximately eighteen different mental health diagnoses, I don't know why it happens or how to stop it. It's like having the *Reservoir Dogs* crew stuck in my mind and on the rampage 24/7. I inhabit some weird fantasy world, a place that's detached from reality as much as possible, where *everything* is cause for anxiety and panic and where, despite often overwhelming evidence to the contrary, my mind insists that living in a fantasy world like this, even such a shitty, noisy one, is better than acknowledging and accepting the happier reality of my existence.

It's a drug, you know, fantasy; Freud thought it was a defence, Klein a projection and Jung, well, thank fuck for Jung. He thought it was healthy – a pathway to creativity. I don't know what's true any more. But what I do know is that, for all the negative effects (dissociation, memory loss, avoidance, fucked-up relationships, anger, loneliness, isolation), fantasy is also what helps keep me alive. It's there for soothing and creating. A comfort blanket. And it almost invariably uses music as its backbone.

Ever since I was a kid I knew what music meant. I *felt* how it tunnelled into me, underneath words and reason, and made everything better. There is nothing more universal than music and the inner worlds it grants us access to. Music is, for me and for all of us, an entirely natural language more powerful, believable and authentic than words.

I'm saying it again because it's worth repeating a second – even a hundred – times: there is nothing more universal than music. It's why E.M. Forster said music was 'the deepest of the Arts, deep beneath the Arts'. It transcends language and culture and wealth and religion, and burrows deep inside us beneath all the shit. Ironically, as it expresses itself within us in that non-verbal, hidden part of ourselves, it allows us to express ourselves better on the outside. One of life's great gifts is that we are all born fluent in a second language. This language, music, is our birthright. Music is a life-saving, life-enhancing, staggeringly profound phenomenon. Even more so because it is entirely inexplicable – as elusive to reason and logic as it is imbued with comfort and a sense of the miraculous.

And while everyone from north London to Goa is eating their raw food, browsing the 'self-development' section on Amazon and having their caffeine enemas in an attempt to get some meaning injected into their lives, the biggest revelation to me is that these guys – Bach, Beethoven, Chopin, Schubert, Brahms, Rachmaninov and the rest – *invented* mindfulness. You don't need a squadron of bald, commando monks tying you down in a forest and chanting *at* you to find inner peace and meaning, you just need to learn how to shut the fuck up, plug in some decent headphones and escape into yourself while listening to the most immortal music ever written.

So yes, amongst other things, this book is also about the music that I love.

Classical music.

Every time I write that phrase, I feel an apology coming on. The (entirely undeserved) reputation it has got (thanks to so many of the people who inhabit that rarefied world and are so fiercely intent on preserving it for a certain 'type' of person) now makes saying you listen to it and enjoy it seem almost like a confession. But I will confess happily. Because this music, this immortal, genius, timeless, magical music that keeps me balanced and able to function, is everything to me. And listening to it, reading about it, playing it may not be a definitive cure, but it sure as fuck supersedes all the myriad other methods I have tried over the years to help calm me down and lift me up. And there have been a *lot* of other methods.

It's no coincidence that the specific pieces I write about in this book are mostly all about fantasy. There are two big works by Chopin that both have the word 'fantasy' in the title – pieces of music that belong almost to a dream world, where Chopin is able to find some semblance of control over his external world through music, even if in reality that world is falling apart; a late Beethoven sonata that reveals a hidden, profoundly deep inner world and has an almost religious fantasy feel to it; shorter works by Bach and Rachmaninov and Gluck that are all, for me, essentially about escaping reality and immersing ourselves in another dimension.

These are the pieces I played at every concert during the five-month tour I did in 2016. And given that, this journal largely involves either:

- being alone in various hotels, ranging from hellholes to luxury refuges, consumed by the voices in my mind, or
- hanging out with whichever poor soul is acting as my tour manager and has to put up with my retarded eating habits, while I fight with the voices in my mind, or
- shuffling onto a stage on my own in front of anywhere between 100 and 2,500 people I have never met, doing my best to suppress the voices in my mind.

You get the idea. It's not so much about being on the road, it's more about avoiding being run over by the sixteen-wheeler that is my head and ending up as roadkill. And so, inevitably, this book is also sometimes about my attempts at head management

– something it needs alarmingly often. My hope is that out of all the madness will emerge a road map of sorts, a way to navigate ourselves through the hustle and bustle of the daily grind.

A traditional self-help book (which this most certainly is not) would prescribe regular affirmations for someone with my particular brand of crazy. Positive statements that we're meant to repeat out loud throughout the day, usually while standing in front of a mirror. 'Mirror-work', they call it. The problem being that – somewhat obviously, I feel – genuinely happy people do *not* stand in front of their mirrors yelling about how happy they are. And no, affirmations don't purify the mind or activate the brain's reward centre, or anything like that. All they do is remind us of how appallingly we're falling short of impossible standards. They sound for the most part like vomit is coming out of our mouths rather than actual words. I've put some typical ones at the start of each chapter for you to mull over. And then I've translated them into normal. These translations are, I hope, slightly more realistic and authentic, even if they're not always pretty.

They're there because they're true and they reflect honestly how I was feeling at that time; that's the only way I think I can jettison the wild, quite mad ramblings of my mind – get them out in the open and meet and greet them head-on.

One last thing: I encourage you – beg you, even – to download, stream, even *buy*, some of the music I write about in this book. Watch YouTube videos, buy a Lang Lang CD,[1] go on Spotify, stream/download my recording of these tour pieces if I ever manage to record it. I don't care who you listen to playing these compositions; I just want you to hear them.

They might, just might, change your inner world forever.

---

1 Don't buy a Lang Lang CD

AFFIRMATION 1:

'The universe holds me, nurtures
me and protects me. Love and
peace flow from me and to me
in perfect harmony.'

TRANSLATION:

'I AM A PARANOID, MOODY AND ANGRY PIECE OF SHIT,
AND ANGER KEEPS ME ALIVE. FUCK YOU.'

Bach Prelude in C Major

If I ever travelled back in time and met Bach, I don't know if I'd punch him or blow him.

This is the man who created some of the most perfect, miraculous, life-changing music the world has ever known and singlehandedly altered the course of musical history for three centuries and counting. Hence the blow job. And yet, far too frequently, he would write at the top of his manuscripts, J.J. (short for *Jesus juva*, or 'Jesus help me'), or, at the end, *Soli deo gloria* ('for the glory of God'). 'It is God who makes the music,' he declared, a little bit too often. This near-constant humble apology for his talent makes me incandescent with rage. Hence the punch. I just wish he had enough self-esteem to swagger a little bit and own what he accomplished rather than naming/ blaming some mysterious intangible entity as the source of it all.

He once wrote, 'The aim and final end of *all* music should be none other than the glory of God and the refreshment of the soul.' There we go again with the bullshit God routine. It's

11

frustrating, right? But the refreshment of the soul, on the other hand . . . Sign me up.

Imagine for a moment living through a childhood from hell, experiencing a degree of loss and grief that most of us will never know and *still* dedicating your life to refreshing other people's souls. Bach has such an unjust reputation as some nerdy, dry, asexual, religious nut-fuck. As a composer of music that is cold, mathematical, unromantic, dull, overly complicated.

I talk a lot about Bach's life, and I should do it a lot more because it is as inspiring as it is awesome. There is no doubt that he was a complex man. From very early on in his life it must have become clear to him that the world is a festering shithole of disappointment and loss. The guy still ended up a senior in school at the age of fourteen when all the other seniors were nearly eighteen. And this despite (or perhaps because of) the fact that he had been orphaned by the age of ten and was living with an older brother who didn't want him and went to a school that treated him like a punchbag. Hence, perhaps, the self-esteem issues.

So desperate was he to learn about music that he stole a volume of scores by leading composers that his brother wouldn't let him have out of spite, and painstakingly copied the book by moonlight (they were too poor to use candles) over a period of months, to the point that he seriously injured his eyes. Possibly the only teenager in history to nearly go blind from studying rather than wanking.

At fourteen he realised that living with his brother was untenable – there was no money, too many other kids (his brother's own children, not burdens foisted upon him the way Bach himself was), too much violence. So he set off and walked 200 miles to a school in Luneburg where he threw himself into studying.

Walked.

At fourteen!

This is the kind of person we're dealing with here. A man who would later spend a month in jail because he tried to quit a job that didn't allow him the musical freedom he so desperately wanted. A man who fathered twenty children, composed more music than almost any other composer in history, duelled, drank, boned groupies and who, in addition to his parents and many of his siblings, endured the loss of eleven of those twenty children, as well as his deeply loved wife. Who, despite these horrors, refused to crumble like so many of us would, and fought, through music, to stay alive and help others. He poured those feelings of rage, hurt, betrayal, love, despair, grief, surrender and, unbelievably, hope into his music on a daily basis.

You want to know the recipe for genius? Take all the notes on a piano keyboard, some manuscript paper, a pencil and the most basic key of C major. Mix together with thirty-five musical bars for a little under two minutes, shake well and pour out a gentle, lilting, seemingly uncomplicated little prelude based on a simple, apparently predictable, repeated pattern of notes.

That's how Bach ended up with the first of forty-eight preludes (with their respective fugues) that are today studied by all music students everywhere, that Chopin played every morning before breakfast for inspiration, that can be played in a crowded room and within a few seconds bring everyone to awestruck silence. That first C major prelude of his is a master-class in simplicity and hidden depths. A lesson in creating something so much greater than the sum of its parts that it's the musical equivalent of splitting the atom. With a much happier explosion. It is a breathtakingly beautiful cascade of notes that strips away everything we think we know, burrows into our souls and allows us all to float away somewhere warm and safe and magical.

Which is just what I need when my mind has been hijacked by the angriest demons on the planet, I'm convinced people are coming after me and there is fire spewing out of my head.

*

MADRID, AUGUST 2016

It's 3.50 a.m., it's concert day and I'm on my knees in a hotel bathroom about to throw up.

The dream I was having jump-started my heart at a rate that feels very nearly fatal. These dreams come almost every night, and if I'm lucky I just let my subconscious get battered without waking up. But this was a particularly bad one.

It was the green room noise that threatened to finish me off. It always does in my dreams (and occasionally in reality). Backstage in every big concert hall they have a speaker mounted on the wall of the green room that transmits the sounds from the auditorium. It starts quietly as people begin to take their seats. The occasional laugh, the odd cough. It builds as mumbling leads to chatter, segueing into a noisy hubbub as more and more people come in. It's a crescendo of evil. This is when I start to think about pulling the fire alarm, calling in a bomb threat, putting my hand through a glass window. In this dream I stupidly don't do any of these things.

Instead I walk, a lamb to the slaughter, onto the stage where there is a huge symphony orchestra assembled and 3,000 people applauding and waiting. The orchestra is ready to play Rachmaninov's 3rd Piano Concerto with me as the soloist. The only problem being it's a piece I have never learned or played. But for some reason – mainly because, like me, my dreams are oftentimes incomprehensibly stupid – I'm sure it'll be OK. I'm apprehensive but figure that somehow, magically, when I sit down, the notes will come.

Only they don't. Of course they don't. Because we're in my very twisted head and not in some Disney film. I'm lost after four bars and the audience starts braying and mocking and laughing, and the conductor, mortified, is looking at me in a panic as still the orchestra plays on. I don't know what I'm doing, my stiff hands are spastically hitting the keyboard and making the musical equivalent of ultra-niche sex noises. Then I just start shouting at the top of my lungs, screaming, jets of incomprehensible black madness shooting out of my mouth and out of the crown of my head as I open my eyes in my hotel room, heart pounding, skin stinking and slick, vomit rising in my throat as I stumble into the bathroom.

After cleaning myself up, I reach for the light. I am in the middle of an ambush and it's not safe to go back to sleep. For the hundredth time that week I am weak with gratitude for cigarettes. I smoke illegally at the window of my hotel, nicotine doing its thing, the city of Madrid silent and peaceful, the antithesis of me.

My muscles are sore, my head feels like it's about to explode. It takes an hour for me to start to relax. I constantly try to remind myself of what's real and what isn't (the perennial challenge when alone in the middle of the night) and try to focus on my breathing.

I think about how my mind works, how I lose perspective and forget things all the time, as if there's a finite amount of space in there and sometimes there is just so much shit that lots of the other stuff (much of it good) is getting booted out and evicted to make room for more crap, more lies, more self-hatred. There is a constant voice in my head. There are several, in fact. A whole committee of them. A shitty committee. They argue, debate, rage, criticise, occasionally reassure, evaluate, dissect, analyse and plan twenty-four hours a day with military precision.

I do wonder what those voices are. Where they come from. Faulty wiring? Defective hardware? They are ever-present and have been since childhood. There was a brief time as an adult when they seemed to quieten down somewhat, but the legal battle waged over the publication of my first book awakened them with a vengeance. Imagine finally speaking out fully and openly about something as messed up and personal as having been raped as a child and almost losing your home, your bank account (final legal bills were approaching £2,000,000), your career and your sanity as a result? Me, some schmuck from north London who plays the piano was, albeit inadvertently, the figure behind the most important legal case in publishing in a century. It's being taught in law schools around the world now and is officially called The Rhodes Case. Me. Go figure. It's like having a disease named after you rather than an action figure. And much though it pains me to admit it, to give it even more power, I think it changed me definitively for the worse. My psychiatrist explained it to me as 'trauma on top of trauma in an eighteen-month-long loop'. In fact, I'm pretty sure it set me back a decade or so.

But we won in the end (I'm pathetically grateful to the Supreme Court).

The book eventually came out and sold well enough. It made it into the *Sunday Times* bestseller list. It got translated into a dozen languages. More, maybe. At the time of writing it's been in the top ten in Spain for months. There's going to be a movie made (no more lawyers, I'm begging you). And while all this is happening I'm touring, learning new piano pieces, recording new albums, presenting radio shows, writing things for the papers, doing press stuff and interviews, making documentaries, writing more books and trying to keep my feet on the ground and stay content. Because this is everything I've always wanted. A life surrounded by, engulfed by, music. After working my ass off, a healthy dose of good luck and a lot of help, that is what I now have.

But these voices are still there. It makes me question how I survived and made it this far. Honestly I don't know how any of us manage to survive and endure. Because have you met anyone, ever, who wouldn't be diagnosed with *something* from the DSM-V (the diagnostic manual used by psychiatrists around the world to put a label on our crazy), even if it's just mild social anxiety or occasional low mood? How are we all somehow managing to function amidst the noise and haste? How can we become mentally well, even just mentally OK, in a world where almost all of us are mentally ill? For so many of us it's a fucking jungle out there.

It might seem obvious to you, but it is extraordinary to me that my mood, my ability even to stay alive, let alone stay healthy or happy, is controlled entirely by my own thoughts. Like many of us, those thoughts don't seem to be dependent on what is actually happening in the outside world, they don't care for facts, they have no concept of reality other than the mind's own special version of it. And the source of its information for this reality is the exact opposite of well-balanced, objective, intelligent or kind. My mind has created, and continues to create, its own distorted yet ultra-convincing truth. Most of the time, everywhere I look, I see danger, fire, threats. They vary according to which voice in my head is shouting the loudest.

It's exhausting.

I stub out another cigarette on the hotel window ledge. Flush the evidence down the loo.

I go back to bed, manage to fall asleep fitfully, and wake up again at 7.30 a.m. The sheets cling to me and my skin smells of decaying sweat once more. Even this early, Madrid is hotter than hell. I lie there, sweltering, thinking about how I shouldn't even be here in the first place. The offer to give a concert in this city came in weeks ago and I declined it because I was meant to be on holiday, but they kept calling and kept pushing, and Denis – my manager – and the promoters and everyone else kept insisting how important it was (like any gigs aren't important) and how I needed to say yes to it. So I did. Because I'm spineless and what if they're right and who am I to turn things down and I need the money and maybe I'll meet a nice girl and it's an amazing venue and the Spanish are so fucking lovely and I know my pieces and why not and it might be really fun you never know.

Of course, now I'm here I feel angry and resentful. I have no autonomy any more. I think back to the conversation Denis and I had about this gig. He has this really irritating tendency to happily agree with me on something, knowing full well he can then talk me round to do whatever the hell he thinks I should do.

'I just really need a clear two weeks off to rest and recover and prepare for September onwards,' I whined at him.

'Couldn't agree more. Try and take all of August. You deserve it, champ!' he said.

And then he called back the next day.

'Look, maybe we should rethink this one. It's just, you know how important it is. Normally I'd totally support you in taking some time off but, well, it's being organised by the mayor of Madrid and I'm worried that if we turn this one down it may have a pretty big impact. Just think about it. No pressure, I'll support you 100 per cent whatever you decide, but let's chat more tomorrow about it once you've had a think.'

Yeah. He'll support me 100 per cent. As long as I do whatever the fuck he thinks is right for me. They all play such a good game. The ex-wives (still can't get used to the fact that I need to use the plural) promising they'll love me for ever, the friends swearing they're there all the time at the end of the phone, the journalists' seemingly innocent off-the-record questions, the lawyers saying their latest bill is entirely justified, the publishers wanting another book exposing my idiotic fucking head because it's a brave (read 'freak show') thing to do and really they just fucking want what they want and, like me, will do whatever it takes to get it.

This is what the voice in my head is telling me right now. I'm sinking rapidly down the hole and into the 'trust no one' void. Repeat in the mirror ten times: 'I am a paranoid, moody and angry piece of shit, and anger keeps me alive. Fuck you.'

I wander down and out to the closest café. Ask for a coffee and a croissant. The voice of furious suspicion is still in charge. The waiter despises me. He knows I'm English. Too lazy to learn Spanish. Orders the wrong thing. Adds ketchup to everything. No doubt it's going to be more expensive than it would be for the next, local guy who orders it.

When I was younger I was extremely paranoid. I was frequently convinced my car had been bugged and that people were following me. Every conversation could potentially be recorded and used as evidence. Still today I often look around to see if I am being followed or whether I notice the same person twice; I have a shortcut to a voice recorder app on my phone's home screen so I can record anything I might need to use as evidence; I regularly screenshot messages and emails for the same reason. Why? Because in my head, when the paranoia takes over, I imagine the worst: therapists are looking for an excuse to section me; one-night stands are waiting for the right time to accuse me of having forced them to have sex; lawyers want to wring more and more money out of me; Denis wants to earn more and move on and look after other artists who aren't psycho.

When I'm thinking like this I need to take constant precautions to plan and protect myself. 'Be prepared' isn't just a motto; it's essential to survival, a way of life. My computer has encryption software, VPNs, and is routinely wiped and restored to factory settings. My worst fear is if I die and someone finds and accesses my laptop (despite a twenty-seven-character password, two-step authentication and fingerprint security). Nobody can know me. See the internet history, read my notes, my draft emails, my real thoughts. They're too disturbing. Amusingly there's not even any niche porn on there. Just words. My authentic self. My everyday searches, random lists, diary entries, digital footsteps and random assorted thoughts. And God forbid if anybody were to see that, to see the real me. I am always both shocked and awed by those who are able to keep a proper paper journal without password protection.

No surprise, then, that I think I recognise a guy at another table from the airport the previous evening. I glare at him. Like I'm in some low-budget spy movie and I totally know what he's doing. I *know* you, motherfucker. Fuck off. Stop following me. Stop watching me.

I smoke *at* him. Cram food into my face defiantly. The waiter who so obviously hates my guts comes up to me. I know I'm going to have to leave. But then I see he's holding a Spanish copy of *Instrumental*. He smiles at me and tells me, in unbelievably good English, that his girlfriend gave him my book a few days ago and he can't stop reading it. Which is why he has it at work. He is really sorry to bother me but would I mind signing it. He wants me to dedicate it to her. Because he clearly adores her.

A part of me just melts. That this guy would want that from me, would rate me highly enough to ask me this. Me. This awkward, lonely freak. I don't understand it, but I have to believe him because he's right there in front of me and has no reason to lie. Of course I sign it and ask him if he wants a photo and we share a selfie together. I soften and feel a little bit less itchy to look at.

I pay the bill, overtip for love's sake, and decide to head back to the hotel. The guy I was so sure had been following me is forgotten. For a brief moment there is a spring in my step.

It doesn't last. I get back to the hotel. Draw the blinds. Text Denis saying I've got a tonne of work to do and prepare for nine hours on my own, Netflix for company, before I need to go to the concert venue. Invisible, hidden, safe. I am so tetchy and fearful of others that I need to shut everyone out. A shrink once told me that I am an island. I assume that we are all like that to an extent, breathing more easily in solitude than in front of others. Of course it struck home immediately. I belong somewhere, marooned and inaccessible. And when I'm like this, if a boat *should* appear to rescue me I'll set fire to it and kill everyone on board. Because fuck you all. There's a reason I have an immediately accessible 'go bag' at home with cash in pounds, euros and dollars, a burner mobile, my second passport and a few clothes. The ability to escape from any situation at a moment's notice is a necessity not a luxury.

Problem is, hiding solves nothing when I'm this angry, because the anger inevitably turns inward, which, let's be honest, is what it's all about anyway. I don't need people around me to feel like an aberration; in fact I can do it much better on my own. I know that there's always a con, that no situation will ever be truly safe and that 'trust no one' is the only piece of advice that matters. And by 'no one' I include myself. Most of all, I can never trust myself. I don't know why I feel like the world is against me, but I do not question the veracity of that information.

I watch an episode of *Stranger Things*. Immediately start watching another one. And another. Doing Netflix shots.

A girl I've been on a couple of dates with messages me that she's missing me. My read receipts are on (nope, I've no idea why I have them turned on either) and she therefore knows I've seen her message. I need to figure out if her message ('I miss you, how are things?') is genuine (of course it isn't), what it is she wants in response (reassurance and a compliment), why she's saying these things in the first place (no fucking idea), what I am going to send back and when (too many options here) and a massive panic ensues. I go online and see – because Mr Paranoid here is always looking for evidence – that she's instagrammed some racy pictures that were clearly taken by someone else. They're not overtly sexual, but I've decided they're definitely, irrefutably early morning, which tells me she's definitely, irrefutably had some guy over for the night, they've fucked and whatever she's told me about wanting to be with me is a line and nothing more. Which is clearly the rational conclusion.

There are so many questions to unpack here. Most urgent is that fact that she knows what time I read her message. So do I want to make her wait or do I reply straight away? And for that I need to know what I want – do I want her to think I'm totally into her or do I want to be more distant?

But I can never be distant. I can't wait and just let things hang, especially any kind of message. If an email or a text isn't replied to within a minute of me seeing it then my whole world will implode. So I have to be quick now and get a response back to her. I know that she's after something and that she will, at some point, fuck me over. I need to prepare for that but still be able to get something out of the situation before the fucking-over occurs. In this case, sex, an escape from loneliness and a temporary boost to my self-esteem.

The problem is that my mind is still telling me that everything I say to her is potential ammunition. For the inevitable break-up, for her lawyers, to put on Twitter, to tell her friends and family, to score point after point. It's draining monitoring everything.

So I tap into my phone something trite and insincere ('You too kiddo. A lot!') with a couple of millennial-friendly emojis and go back to trying to lose myself in pixels. This is the closest I get to escape, but it's no good, I now really can't concentrate on Eleven and the monster. All because of a six-word text.

I need to get out of the room again; it's not doing me any good being here with my thoughts. It's creeping up to lunchtime anyway. Well, from a British perspective at least. I saunter down the Gran Via. It's crazy-inducing hot (have I mentioned this already?). I'm looking for somewhere fast, easy, where I won't feel like a cunt for eating alone. Not that I want anyone with me right now – I am actually weak with relief at not having to try and be a normal, balanced adult in front of someone. We're busy enough trying to manage my dissociative identity disorder (diagnosis no. 12). The pressure of having a girlfriend here would be just too much to take right now. Having to put the mask on and be the me they think they know is exhausting when I'm in this kind of state. I'd have to engage with them, buy them things because that's what is expected if they're to stay with me, listen to them, remember stuff, feign interest, when all the time a darker part of my mind would just want to throw them under a bus.

I find myself at a place that has pictures on the menu instead of words. It suits me just fine. I point and mumble, ashamed of myself, light up and feel the sun burning into my skin. As soon as the food arrives it disappears. In the past five years, I've not once had a meal lasting longer than forty-five minutes. And this one doesn't even last a quarter of that before cash is left on the table and I'm scurrying off in the heat like a beaten dog.

I find myself on the Calle del Barquillo and see a sign for the Prado museum. Something tells me to start heading in that direction. A hidden calling from that better part of me to do something, anything, worthy while I'm here. And it's got to be air conditioned. But the real reason is that there is a certain cloak of invisibility from the crowd that suits me for now – I can pretend to fit in with other people and see if that stops me feeling lonely, lifts my mood, kills the voice of negativity. I arrive and see the throngs of Japanese tourists, eager students, bored children and the odd individual like me: hot, jaded, remote, joining queues solely for the human interaction, while remaining reassuringly anonymous.

I work my way to the front, avoid the main attraction (something called Bosco) and head to the quieter part of the museum. It is, the guy at the door reliably informs me, the largest museum in the world, just before he offers me a tour for €40. I really want to say yes, because I know nothing about art and what an opportunity this would be to learn something . . .

'No, thank you,' I mumble dismissively, and walk away quickly.

But as I do so, I take a museum plan from his hand. Looking at it I feel that perhaps my feet have brought me here for a reason. There is a painting that I've read about over the years but never seen, one that has always resonated with me, and it's right there on the map.

El Coloso.

By Goya. The painting equivalent of Beethoven.

Goya and Beethoven lived around the same time, and each went deaf at around the same time too. They both initially worshipped and then despised Napoleon, survived the French Revolution and spent too much of their lives depressed. They were socially retarded, angry, mistaken for/actually were homeless bums, didn't give a fuck and blew up their respective art forms with buckets of C4 explosive, dragging it by the scruff of the neck from Classical into Romantic. I figure if there's one artist I can respect, understand, want to get to grips with, then it's Goya, especially as one of the rooms on the way to *El Coloso* contains his *Pinturas negras* – 'The Black Paintings'. That very much speaks to me (paging Dr Freud). The room itself is large, cool, and feels charged. It is, oddly, almost completely empty of people, and I walk to the centre of it and spin slowly in a full 360.

There are fourteen paintings depicting Goya's visions of evil and hell and everyday life (constructs that are to him clearly indistinguishable from one another). It's almost too much to take in. There's a dog drowning, people getting eaten, old men with distressed and disturbed faces fighting over scraps of food . . . The sheer horror of it, the vile, ugly emotions from all these scenes of rape, war and shame engulf me. At the same time, it's utterly captivating. I'm witnessing this, inhaling it in a voyeuristic way that isn't seedy but rather enlightening. Death, destruction and hurt. What makes up our majority.

Then, just outside that room I see the *Coloso*. A giant rising up above the masses and scaring the shit out of the peasants. Easily as shattering as Beethoven's *Eroica* Symphony or his 'Hammerklavier' Sonata. It's magnificent. It mirrors perfectly the darker side of Beethoven – that kind of terrible wonder. A canvas bleeding with desolation, disillusion, pain and heartache with its bleak colours and coarse textures.

It all gets a bit too much for me. In any event I suddenly notice the security guards staring at me uneasily as if they think I'm going to lick the canvas and shit on the floor. I don't really belong here.

I'm exhausted. I know instinctively that the kindest thing I can do for myself now is to catch up on some badly needed sleep before I head to the venue for my soundcheck. I walk in the heat back to the hotel. The do not disturb sign hits the door and I lie, fully clothed, on the bed, the air conditioning on full blast. In my head is only the music I'm going to play tonight, running through on a never-ending loop. Sometimes it is the only way sleep is possible. Words are dangerous, music is salvation – the one thing I don't need to be afraid of. My force field. I slow things down, playing the pieces through in my mind at a fraction of the normal speed, a mental musical metronome tick-tocking rhythmically and gently. I feel my heart rate start to ease up, my pulse dropping, eyes getting heavier, muscles starting to relax. This is my best place – the hinterland between wake and sleep where things are warm, fuzzy, not quite defined. I allow myself to drift deeper into myself and away from the real world. Grateful, safe, cocooned.

I come round with the help of my alarm after a couple of hours and have no clue where I am. No dreams, no nightmares this time. As reality slowly filters back into my brain, I gulp down a bottle of water and start to panic. Time is running out here at the hotel and soon I'll need to be out and about, rehearsing, checking out the venue, waiting backstage, dealing with people. All I really want to do is completely avoid interacting with anyone, walk straight from the hotel to the stage, not utter a single word, play, come back to the hotel, eat alone and pass out. But I can't do that.

The voice of paranoia is bubbling up again to the surface of my mind. Worst of all, I find myself thinking, no, *knowing*, that I have no right to be here in the first place. Not on a stage with a piano. Not at a sold out concert. Not playing Bach and Chopin and Beethoven – these pieces that ever since I was a child I have worshipped, inhaled and stayed alive for. The voice is so loud that I convince myself that I am perpetuating a fraud. And although most of the audience are too naive to know it, *I* know it. The promoters know it. The critics know it. Other musicians, piano teachers, seasoned concert-goers, even family and close friends know it. But nevertheless I have thrown myself at this choice of career with all the neediness and desperation with which you seize a life preserver after you've thrown yourself overboard and suddenly realise it was a really shitty idea. At every concert I definitely catch sly winks, smirks, unspoken signals from various people. They know.

I get changed and wander across the street to the venue, the Fundación Francisco Giner. It is conveniently close, a short walk, head down, heart pounding. As I walk through the backstage door, closer to the piano, I begin to feel slightly better. I relax a little. It's as if these lovely ghosts of the great composers are waiting for me to take on their mantle and keep them alive in 2016. Even that they're happy for me to do so. The promoter and Denis are there. As is the hall manager. They take me into the hall itself and for a moment I forget my fear, because it is magnificent. It's like a spaceship, the bastard offspring of Zaha Hadid and Frank Lloyd Wright.

The piano itself is *huge* on the smallish stage; God knows how they got it in there. I sit down and let Denis deal with the technical guys while I disappear and focus on the only important thing – the sound. It really is a wonderful piano. A Steinway model D, the best of the best. It feels a bit like sitting on a musical superbike, hard and powerful and, with a split-second lapse of concentration, deadly. Music-making *should* feel deadly on occasion (with a healthy dose of perspective of course – it's clearly not disaster-relief work or brain surgery). But it should be about taking risks and giving everything to it rather than playing it safe and steady. As I practise, that feeling I had inside me as I walked in of wanting to be there, of believing I can do this, of feeling so goddam excited that I am about to reach back two or three-hundred years and offer up these unbelievable pieces to an audience, begins to grow. This is my very own musical retreat. A sanctuary.

It is startling how my head can take me down to one extreme and then up to another so quickly, like some kind of uncontrollable elevator in a David Lynch-designed shopping mall.

I work through some slow passages to get a better feel for the piano. The weight of the keys, the depth of the sound, the pedals. Lights are constantly going on and off and changing colour, but I don't notice anything other than the sound. It's substantial but intimate, like a really hot girl sighing into your ear as she comes.

(Whatever, it's my book; I'll use any fucking analogy I want.)

What comes out of the instrument fills the room completely. More importantly it fills me. That part of me that nothing else can fill in these moments.

After twenty minutes or so I know the piano well enough. I've made friends with it. Her, maybe. Denis and I and the tech guys spend another ten minutes fixing the lights (it's remarkably hard to get rid of the shadows on the keyboard, something that's essential as fingers have to be millimetre accurate on the keys and any darkness/contrast throws off visual perspective) and checking the microphone – it's important to have a barely noticeable difference between the volume of my voice when I speak to the audience and the volume of the opening piece of music I'll be playing after introducing it so that everything seems even. And then we're set.

I feel nervous. Tonight I'm playing two pieces in public for the first time: the Bach prelude and the Beethoven sonata.

The best thing for me is to slink backstage to my green room, to be alone and quiet, to focus and munch on bananas and nuts and play (Scrabble) with myself. To make sure that I am in control of the situation so that this moment never, ever turns into one of my green room nightmares. But evidently there are other plans. Three TV news networks want to interview and film me playing. It's 8 p.m. Doors open at 8.30. The concert starts at 9. I'm hungry and hot. I feel the anger rising again.

I'm angry at Denis, who is supposed to insulate me from all this shit, especially just before a concert. He is busy convincing me to squeeze in an extra radio interview on top of the rest of it and telling me that it's fine and will take fifteen minutes max. But it isn't fine. It's just another fucking thing to do for other people when all I want to do is disappear and go inside of myself.

Of course I agree because I've no spine and maybe, just maybe, Denis is being sensible and it really isn't a big deal. Right?

So off I pop. Back on the stage. Back at the piano. Dancing like a monkey. Trying to think of pieces and sections I can play that will impress the journalists (I'm shallow like that) and also move them (I'm needy like that). Of course it's not just fifteen minutes like they promised. Microphones don't work, batteries need changing, interpreters don't understand, and before I know it I'm hustled off stage at 8.40 p.m., the doors are opened, the concert will start late and it's only now that I'm finally alone and waiting in my green room.

I'd taken some pills earlier and they must be working their magic, because my hands are no longer shaking and my heart rate isn't spiking. I always take them seventy-five minutes before a gig starts. Propranolol. It saves my ass on stage – a beta blocker that suppresses the physical symptoms of adrenalin (try playing Chopin with shaking hands, sweaty palms and trembling legs) but has no impact at all on the mental side of things. Lots of people in the industry take it. None of them talk about it. Taboo. Because, you know, we're meant to be machines who can do everything perfectly all the time without any pharmaceutical help. Which is bullshit. Hendrix dropped acid. Kurt Cobain brought a bottle of wine on stage with him. I can take a fucking pill if it'll help me play better.

There's the slight tingling of nerves in my teeth and gums and stomach, but after a few deep breaths a cloud of warmth settles over me, and for pretty much the first time this day I am still and quiet, and not spooked and startled. The audience noise from the loudspeaker, the one that plagues me in the nightmares, doesn't even bother me. Everyone has gone; all I'm waiting for is the sweet Spanish girl to come get me when they're ready to start the show. It's so full that they can't get everyone in and seated and so the start time is pushed back even more, but I don't even care now. I'm just thinking about the first bars of the Bach prelude I'm opening with.

It's always a big moment when I'm playing something in front of an audience for the first time. It's the strangest thing, but I could play as well as any living pianist in this hall when it's empty. Just me, the piano, the music and I would fly effortlessly. But put one single person in the room to listen and everything changes. I've never understood it. I know rationally that nothing has really changed, and yet still that sudden risk of exposure, of looking like a fool in front of other people and feeling shame is enough to force me to rely absolutely on every single one of those 20,000-plus hours of practice and use every trick in the book to try and manage my head and the voices.

The girl comes in and ushers me to the side of the stage. The lights go down, the audience quietens, the voice of God (West End speak for the pre-show 'doors to manual, we are about to take off' stuff) forbids photography and cellphones and then, suddenly, there's the Spanish version of 'Ladies and gentlemen, please welcome to the stage, Mr James Rhodes', I walk on (bounce on perhaps), lights are brighter than expected, I bow (well, nod my head slightly because I'm shy and haven't done anything yet that deserves a proper bow), noting random, smiling faces in the crowd, and sit down at the piano. Lights go down almost to zero. There is enough for me to see the keys but everything else is in darkness. I close my eyes and take a breath and count to five in my head. Ten is too long. Five just enough to centre.

Off I go, starting with the gentle C major arpeggio that opens the Bach prelude. These 120 seconds contain at some level all the secrets of the universe. How something so seemingly simple can be so deceptively deep will always baffle me. But as I move through the bars, floating from C major down into more and more harmonically murky waters, I allow it to take me over and carry me away safely. This is why I do this. Right that second I'm in total agreement with Bach: here is proof of God's existence. The whole day of shit and worry and anxiety melts away and I'm left lying by the ocean, loved and held.

There is something so immensely satisfying in playing this piece. The patterns of notes stay the same, and so on the OCD scale (another attractive speciality of mine, more of which later), it really hits the spot. That repetition and the ability to sink deep into the keyboard and get your fingers working, digging, pushing, the multiple hidden melodies within it that can appear or not depending on which notes you decide to give added weight to, the solidity of the harmonies, the dialogue and questions and answers contained within it, the freedom to choose whatever speed and volume you fancy each and every time you play it, the deep, deep romance of this piece, the magic trick of having a bunch of structured, simple semiquavers and using them to create an entire brave new world in an apparently effortless way. The unassailable fact that these thirty-five bars of music make the world a better place and, like some kind of soul alchemy, can effortlessly turn shit into gold.

I am so convinced by this magic, so delighted by it, that I wrote a book showing anyone and everyone how to play it. On the assumption that given the choice, anybody would say yes to being able to play a two-minute piano piece that could get them laid/blow their mind/reawaken a long-abandoned passion. It requires forty-five minutes a day, an electric keyboard or piano and the ability to read. That's it. Oh, and ten fingers. It's called, in a stroke of quite staggering marketing genius, *How to Play the Piano*.

I'd got the idea sometime last year when I got an email from a retired Mexican airline pilot. He told me he used to play the piano as a kid but gave it up and had always regretted it. When he retired he read *Instrumental* and, after finishing the book, bought a piano, got a teacher and now plays every day. He signed off by saying 'These are my best days.' Which made me squeal with delight. Some dude the other side of the world is now playing Bach and Beethoven and having a blast doing it because he read my memoir. That feels good.

I kept thinking about it. And the fact that I've lost count of the hundreds of people who have told me the same thing – they used to play piano as a kid, gave it up (because of girls, boys, football, scales, PlayStations, shit teachers, creepy teachers, parental pressure) and now wish they hadn't. So, I figured, why not give them and others the genuine opportunity to play a Bach masterpiece in a few short weeks which could then lead to them getting a teacher and exploring the piano again in more depth. Or at the very least will have them doing something extraordinary and performing a piece written 300 years ago that still blows the greatest minds of our generation in its simplicity, beauty and joy. And every time I get sent a short video by someone who's read the book, practised and learned that prelude I feel something inside me light up.

I finish the prelude feeling grounded and settled. The rest of the gig goes well. It's a good concert. In a perfect world, I'd be heading back to my room now and ordering room service. Last night's broken sleep and today's heightened and fraught emotions have left me shattered. Instead, because I have to, a bunch of us head for dinner. Me, Denis, the promoters. We enter the restaurant and wander over to our table. It's late, like 11 p.m., and I'm not good at things like this. I've had to step out of my little bubble of safety and emerge back into the real world after playing the last encore, and it's a rude awakening. The waiter says hi to us all and I say to him, 'Can you bring me a burger.' He seems baffled as he hasn't given us menus yet and we've not even sat down. But while we were walking in I saw on the menu outside that, together with all the fancy stuff they offer, they do somewhat apologetically offer cheeseburgers too. And I'm hungry and empty in so many ways. So I ask him again and he nods and disappears.

Ten minutes later everyone is still chatting, we still haven't got menus or ordered drinks and I'm losing my shit inside my head because I just need to eat and sleep and can't handle being around people or out in the open right now. But then I see my super-Spanish-cheeseburger-of-love coming and the waiter pops it down in front of me. Everyone at the table seems surprised I've managed to achieve this and, if I'm honest, a little jealous. But I'm not sharing.

Literally six minutes later, I pull a twenty-euro note out of my pocket, put it on the table and, while trying to plaster my sincerest smile on my face, let everyone know that I need to head back to the hotel for some sleep. This feels entirely beyond my control and something I simply have to do. I can't help it, especially after a day like the one I've just been through. Enter a restaurant with a bunch of people, order and eat, preferably within ten to fifteen minutes, pay, leave, escape, hide. Denis, bless him, gets this and he just smiles. The promoters seem disappointed and uncomfortable, and I get the feeling that, coming from a wonderful culture where food is sacred, and having taken the time to pick a restaurant with a gastro-fuck menu, they'd wanted to stay out for hours talking, planning, discussing, showing off their city.

But I don't get that. No offence intended – I just don't. I know Madrid is spectacular, that it's a city I would give anything to live in, that one day I probably *will* live there at least for a year or two. All I can think of is being somewhere quiet and alone, having time and space to breathe, having a bed to lie down on and go through the concert in my head to try and stop the adrenalin pumping through my body, making notes about what could improve, what could change, what was good, bad or indifferent. I know Denis can sort out any business stuff with them.

I know it seems rude, but it's not. I promise you it's not. It's born of desperation and innocence, not a desire to be a dick even though it often comes across that way. Glenn Gould, arguably the greatest pianist who ever lived and one of my Top Ten Heroes™, got it so right when he talked about there being a ratio of how much time you spend with other people versus how much time you must then spend alone to compensate. I would be very, very happy to spend twenty hours alone for every hour I spend amongst people. I just can't breathe as easily when I'm out in the world. I don't feel safe. There is a biological imperative at work that insists I leave and find safety in much the same way as I would step in front of a bus without hesitation in order to save my son. It's not conscious. It just is. I see people at parties and *know* they're feeling the same thing – 'get me the fuck out of here and put me somewhere where I can just be quiet, alone, not exposed'.

I'm out the door while they sit there still looking at the wine list and deciding what to eat and drink. I make my way back to the hotel, staring at the map on my phone and unable to make head or tail of which way I should be walking (my sense of direction is as effective as my social skills) but I do, eventually, figure it out and reach the welcoming safety of my hotel room.

*

The next morning, 6 a.m., and I'm in a cab on the way to the airport. Denis next to me telling me well done for the show. All I'm thinking about is that prelude. Yesterday's paranoia has morphed into gnawing self-doubt. How much better it could have been. The third finger and thumb of my left hand weren't always completely in time, there were several moments when I put a few grams of extra weight on one of my right-hand fingers when there was no need. So the net effect was that certain passages might have sounded both uneven *and* unbalanced. And then I remember that when this piece was written in 1722, Bach himself wrote that it was 'for the profit and use of musical youth desirous of learning, and especially for the pastime of those already skilled in this study'. Forgetting the youth side of things, I definitely want to learn and I'm also vaguely skilled in this study. So maybe perfection isn't something to aspire to. Perhaps improvement is.

Simple pieces are the hardest to play well. There's nothing to hide behind like you can in the massive chords of a Rachmaninov étude. There are just the notes, sparse and exposed. Then I catch myself considering how many minutes I have spent thinking about, studying and rehearsing this single two-minute piece and I figure it must be at least thirty hours, especially if you take into account my pre-sleep ritual of going over all of my pieces in my head to check my memory. How can one not go slightly mad spending that amount of time obsessing over something? Perfection in creative pursuits isn't tangible anyway, and so it will always fall short. Making music, painting, writing are not equations or formulas that can be solved and proved – they are fluid, subjective, imperfect structures that float into our world and are experienced through our own filters and histories. Perfection to one listener is utterly vile to another.

I remind myself that it's more than likely I was the only person who may have noticed things weren't quite the way I would have wanted them. I always remember learning about 'stroking' at university when doing my B.Sc. in psychology (ironic degree subject of the decade). This idea that all humans, like pets, need not only physical but also emotional stroking at times. Some more than others, maybe, but it's mainly about motivating, reassuring and encouraging ourselves and others, and when we praise or appreciate ourselves or others it's called giving positive strokes.

That's your transactional analysis lesson for the day.

Point is, I need stroking a lot. And I can never get enough of it from outside of myself because when I do get it I don't believe it, so it doesn't count. So I have to, and please excuse me here, stroke myself. Be kind to myself. Reassure myself. Treat myself like I would a toddler who's just had a big, nasty shock. Consistently.

Once when I was tiny I got lost in a shopping mall. I'd wandered off in a daze, and what seemed like hours later I was found. My mum gave me an enormous hug and said, 'Darling, you got lost' and I replied, sobbing, 'Yes and it was a very bad lost.' A very bad lost. Haven't most of us found ourselves in some baffling social situation and felt like they too were in the middle of a very bad lost? And that feeling of being found, being safe and having my feet back on solid ground is what stroking does for me. It's a form of self-soothing and it's becoming more and more second nature.

So I have this mantra that I repeat to myself time and time again: 'It's all OK, it's all OK.' And this counteracts the other intrusive thoughts that pop in there uninvited, like 'Fucking fuck motherfucker fuckity fuck' etc. Somehow the word 'fuck' is very important. Sonically and phonetically it scratches that itch I have that forces me to get the sounds in my head exactly right. But I then get worried that repeating words like that to myself is probably not very good karma and more likely than not it'll just bring a tonne of shit into my life. Sometimes I catch myself doing it and then swap to 'It's OK' again, or 'Love and peace, love and peace' in an attempt to quieten things down and brighten up my world a little bit. Somehow the hard 'p' and soft 'c' manage to soothe things enough, perhaps because it's almost the inverse of the soft 'f' and hard 'k' of fuck. I figure saying 'love and peace' several thousand times a day can't be a bad thing, karmically. I'll let you know if it's working in due course. For the moment it's something that is, and always has been, kind of essential as it allows me to function semi-normally in the outside world without falling apart. On the inside world it's another story. But that's for me to worry about.

I zone back into reality and whatever it is Denis is saying as we get out of the cab. Light up a last cigarette before the hell that is airport security. I have a couple of days at home in London before I need to head off to some other country to do some press and interviews and concerts and talks, and I'm not quite sure what or where or when because it's all a bit over-whelming. I'm frantically typing notes in my diary about what to practise and when and for how much time. Lists keep us all safe. If only I could ever get them just right.

As we board I get an email from the *Guardian* online asking if I'd write an article about the government's child abuse inquiry that has just about completely imploded. I write back 'no' and then two minutes later 'yes' because sometimes you just have to keep talking about things you don't feel comfortable talking about. Even if I'd rather be sleeping on the plane or gazing out of the window thinking about happier things. I write the article at 35,000 feet, all 800 words of it, which is too short to count and too long to be careless with. They come back to me later on saying they have a no swearing policy and they need to remove the line 'all of which leaves me with just one question: what the actual fuck is going on here?' I say no thanks then. Because some things are worth using the word 'fuck' over and this is one of them and it's the *Guardian* after all and not the *Telegraph*, whose readers would have a worse panic attack at 'fuck' than they would at 'immigrant'. The editor reconsiders and lets it run. They even print it, swear word and all, in the next day's hard copy.

I get off the plane with Denis but he is taking his time and wants to go to the bathroom. He always wants to go to the bathroom. It's like a disease for him and it drives me fucking crazy. About to board a plane? Go to the bathroom. About to order food? Bathroom. Just before a gig, in *my* green room? Bathroom. I don't even know what he does in there. I don't want to. And so I just leave him there alone, knowing he'll come out looking for me and I'll already be trying to look innocent in the immigration queue. Because I'm in a rush. Not that there's anything waiting for me at home, just that I'm always in a rush. Because who knows what might happen? I could get a phone call from someone who wants to see me and so I'd need to be in a certain place quickly, I might need to be close to my piano so I can work on a piece I just *have* to work on, the trains could get cancelled or delayed, traffic could suddenly get really bad – basically I just need to get the fuck home from wherever I am as soon as I can so that I feel safe and I won't get trapped anywhere I don't want to be. I know Denis won't mind me abandoning him, just like last night. He knows my weird and is OK with it.

Home I get and, as usual, I hustle through the door and within five minutes am wondering why I hurried so hard to get here. It's empty, and in a depressing way. Divorce does that to a chap. I've been single for a few months. Before you pull the marital plug, despite the initial devastation a small part of you thinks and hopes and even assumes that the immediate future might involve endless hot girls, wild sex, an awesome bachelor pad, more money and more freedom. But, somewhat inevitably, you end up alone, living in a tiny apartment above an all-night chippie where all the drunks go to argue and philosophise in the middle of the night, hating yourself and wanting to scream at strangers on their morning commute because there's nowhere else to let the crazy out.

I open the window, and it's not drunks shouting that I can hear. It's laughter and the clink of glasses, and the faint aroma of hope and good times. The whole world is evidently out doing cool shit.

I look around my sterile little apartment. The fact that I have a night to myself is a blessing, but it also presents a risk that things will spiral downwards. I never really know which way it's going to go, and right now I'm feeling wobbly. I know from experience that the thing that helps suppress the voices and stops me from doing something bad is routine. So I stick to the one I have on nights like this: I run my bath, I download my TV show *du jour*, I turn the oven on and take the loneliest fish pie ready meal for one out of the fridge. I look down at my awkwardly hairy belly as I shuffle back into the bathroom to get my outside clean and kill time and try and remember that everything passes.

But there's something that I'm really not capable of allowing to pass. This one, gnarly, intractable thing. That's what's actually really bugging me right now. And it's not the fact that I used the phrase 'TV show *du jour*'. In the pile of mail when I got back was another threatening letter from some overpriced lawyers. It's the latest in a long line of correspondence from them.

OK. Have you ever got a parking ticket or something similar? Some stupid, irritating, senseless thing that you just cannot let go of? Like it's a fucking tumour, planted there in your head as the greatest injustice in human history? Well, I got this big parking ticket. The A-bomb of tickets. I'll probably go on about it throughout the book. It's not a literal parking ticket, it's a metaphor – which is why from now on I'm going to put it in inverted commas – but it's got that same feeling attached to it of irrational resentment and angry helplessness. Times a billion. So indulge me while I rant and despair and die a little inside about this particular 'ticket'. I can't stop thinking about it as I lie in the water.

Let's stick with the metaphor. I remind myself it could have been a clamp or I could have been towed to a place in that buttfuck part of London that is so shit that no part of Europe would ever want it. My 'car' could even have been removed and destroyed. But, whatever, the reality is I got the 'ticket', and it's driving me crazy with impotent rage. It makes me want to cut myself.

I take a deep breath and try to stop my head going further down this road, to turn the volume down to zero. I've wanted for so many years to find the elusive 'power off' switch to my brain. I'm a long way from finding it, but I recently found a means to temporarily slow things down a little that sometimes works. I always used to wonder, in awe, when I heard people say they could quieten their mind at will or were able to fall asleep within a few minutes. I dated a girl once who could do that – just switch the light off and fall asleep within ninety seconds. I asked her how she managed to do it so goddam quickly. We were lying in bed, I switched off the lights and, as usual, I felt my head starting up like a chainsaw. I say to this girl, who was clearly three seconds away from dropping off into a calm, restful sleep, 'Is your head just quiet right now? What are you thinking about? Do you not have a tonne of thoughts crashing about in there? Aren't you worried about things, thinking about things, planning things, figuring shit out in there?'

'No, not really,' she yawned, 'I just say to myself "It's bedtime now" and then I'm asleep.'

And then, I swear to God, she actually fell asleep. Just like that. With a fucking smile on her face.

As if being alone with your thoughts was no big deal. As if there was an off-switch you could press and then simply shut down for the night like a human computer.

She and I lasted less than a week.

But as I say, I kind of found an off-switch recently. It freaked me out completely because it's the first thing that's ever even semi-worked. Not every time, but often enough for me to feel hopeful. This thing I do is from some New Age audio book my shrink forced me to listen to where an overpaid 'wellness coach' is talking about peace, and he tells you to get quiet, lie down and imagine you're watching your thoughts and just waiting for the next one to come, like a cat watches a mouse hole waiting for the mouse. You ask yourself, 'I wonder what my next thought will be' and wait and listen and watch, really intensely concentrating on looking out for that thought to come.

First time it happened I almost had a heart attack. I was lying down, focusing hard on wondering what my next thought was going to be, and suddenly, for the first time in years, possibly ever, I didn't have any chatter going on in my head. Nothing. The shock was as great as if I'd just started flying. I genuinely didn't think silence inside my head was possible. It's as if my mind is there to confirm that I am indeed alive by causing me intense grief and noisily arguing with itself all the time. Should it ever quieten down then I am convinced it means I'm about to die, and of course that can't happen so, to avoid that, it's set to eleven all the bloody time, *Spinal Tap*-style but without the laughs, and just won't shut up. Since the moment when I heard that audio book, I've managed to get the quiet to last a few minutes at a time. No more than five, but a pretty consistent three or four.

And so I do that. Lying in the bath. Waiting and watching for the next thought, empty and silent in my head. I start to feel better. I stop thinking about the 'parking ticket'. For the first time since I walked through the door of my flat, I am able to believe in an alternate reality for a bit, where I've come home to myself and that home is warm and welcoming. In my imagination there's lovely music on and it smells of roast potatoes and it's got a garden and comfortable furniture and a family where there's actually some 'fun' in the 'dysfunction' and a dog and everything I'd want it to have.

After my bath, I cook my dinner and I watch an HBO show and I feel as still as I'm ever going to feel. I know it won't last, that I've used up my stillness allocation for the day, so I take a Xanax before bed and crash listening to an audio book with the same bullshit life coach talking about the same pseudo-psychological bullshit until I'm away and gone and safe.

This is what thirty-six hours looks like in my head. Welcome to the party.

AFFIRMATION 2:

'I don't need to find my "other half" I am perfectly whole and complete just as I am. A strong, lovable, beautiful human being.'

TRANSLATION:

'YOU COLOSSAL DICKHEAD, YOU HAVEN'T GOT A FUCKING CLUE ABOUT LOVE AND RELATIONSHIPS, YOU'RE GOING TO DIE ALONE AND EVEN YOUR CATS WILL RUN INTO TRAFFIC TO GET AWAY FROM YOU.'

Chopin *Fantasie* in F Minor

Chopin was an asshole. There's no two ways about it. A genius, but an asshole. And yet of all the composers I worship, he is the one I feel the most affinity with. Go figure.

Chopin was weak. Spindly. Scrawny. A man-child. Needy, overly sensitive, petulant and with a giant ego. The ego was justified. He singlehandedly changed piano playing forever. He revolutionised the piano and paved the way for the sound-world we now know it is capable of. He was the first composer to find a way to emulate the human voice using the piano keys – his nocturnes are really songs sung by fingers rather than voices. He invented, or reinvented, entirely new forms (ballades, mazurkas, polonaises, études, nocturnes, scherzos).

Chopin's F minor *Fantasie* is his musical depiction of the fucked-up relationship he had with the writer George Sand. It was an appalling relationship, the worst kind of toxic love. A day with her was too much; a thousand days, never enough. He did all he could to make it work, to be the man he thought she wanted him to be, to impress her, implore her, thrill her and inspire her.

Ultimately, his emotions destroyed him. The relationship ended up literally killing him (broken-heart syndrome masquerading as consumption). But writing this piece allowed him some space to control the chaos. It's a fantasy. He gets to choose exactly how he wants it to play out, like he's in some titty bar back room in South America paying for a hooker to do 'that thing' he can't ask any of his girlfriends to do because they'd stab him and call the police.

This is what I hear when I play it: it starts with Chopin walking up the stairs to a room in the attic where Sand is writing. He knocks at the door and she tells him she's busy. He knocks again. Needy, remember? And again. And then he comes in and they have a gentle chat about things. But by this stage there's no such thing as a gentle chat for long, and she says the wrong thing and he explodes, the bass of the piano thumping down lower and lower while dozens of notes in the right hand go crazy reaching the very top of the keyboard in a frenzy before hurtling down to the very bottom in a fit of fury. But then he realises he's being a colossal dick and tries to make it right. For a while it works and everything feels back on track again. But of course it doesn't last. And throughout this glorious, fifteen-minute piece there are the ups and downs and back and forth and hope and despair and relentless energy that only a big-love dysfunctional relationship can have. It's all there, peeled back and exposed for us all to see – the walking, talking, dancing, fucking, hating, loving, point-scoring, strutting and fighting.

Right at the end, it goes really quiet. Chopin has burnt himself out. Too many thoughts, mind racing too hard, and he just kind of implodes. The music dies down and Chopin writes into the score the melody from a lullaby that his mum used to sing to him when he was a little boy. His musical safety blanket, a way to take him back to the relative safety of childhood. It's astonishing and so intimate and sad. As if he can't carry on as an adult any more, it's just too hard; he so wanted this to work out and he gave it all he had but he wasn't that strong to begin with and now he's half dead, and fuck it's going to kill him.

In so many ways his relationship with Sand was that of a parent and child. She would have him carried up to bed at the same time as her children (literally carried, he was so weak) while she stayed up writing and smoking. She would nurse him, mother him, do all she could to reassure him, and yet, of course, this would lead to unimaginable dysfunction, resentment and hostility.

It was a typical case of asshole meets girl, puts her on a pedestal because he knows deep down he'll never do any better and she seems really cool (George wore trousers and smoked cigars). He thinks she'll be able to fix what's wrong with him, gives her all of him without thinking and without any sense of self or boundaries, and overshares a *lot*. He obviously doesn't get what he expects from her (how could he?), panics, becomes hugely possessive and jealous as a fucked-up defence mechanism, and then seems shocked and betrayed when he ends up alone, miserable and with a hole in his heart the size of a small, war-torn country. She was, of course, also quite a piece of work, playing with him at her leisure, toying with that weird little heart of his and rather enjoying the insanely imbalanced power dynamic.

Chopin was one of the many musicians and composers for whom a relationship in any real sense was an impossibility. While I've never bought into the idea that you have to be messed up and mentally ill to create really worthy things, it's crystal clear that many musicians and artists are perhaps slightly more emotionally skewed than the rest of the world. Or maybe it just seems that way because they're better known and written about more and so their dysfunction follows them about like a foul smell (more likely). Whatever the case, this piece perfectly mirrors my own experience of love – messy, confusing, without any real form, endlessly shifting, filled with both intense beauty and savage pain. I wonder if anyone, ignoring the Disney Channel, has ever, in the whole entire universal history of love, had a relationship that *wasn't* filled with these things. Where the beautiful, intimate, gentle, loving moments are offset and, sadly, sometimes obliterated by the neediness, insecurities and fears that have been lurking underneath all along.

*

MADRID, AUGUST 2016

'Fuck the lot of them' is my middle-of-the-night thought that wakes me up a week later. I'm in a hotel room in Madrid, once more. Sleep disrupted by mental implosion, once more. My eyes pop open, pupils dilated, meth-like, and in my imagination I spring out of bed heading straight for the computer. Lighting a cigarette and opening my mail program at the same time, I start typing furiously.

'You talk about being best friends, about loving me forever, about how I'll always be your one big love and yet look what's happened?! You reassure me that the universe has got my back, that we're still best friends and yet how can that ever be the case given what you've done? Fuck you.'

<Send>

Fuck her.

Slightly regretting that one. Even if it was all just in my head.

That didn't take long. I close my eyes and compose another one on the back of my eyelids:

'I'm so sorry darling. It's 4 a.m. and I've a concert tonight and I miss you and love you and just want you to be OK and us to be OK. I just want the pain to stop. Please delete that last email. Do it for me? We'll figure it out, I promise you. I love you. I miss you. I've made a huge mistake – and I know I'll never find another woman like you.'

<Send>

I'm still drowning in these feelings. Even if they're for someone I haven't been with for years.

Those of you who read *Instrumental* will know that the ending is like a Richard Curtis movie. I am with the woman of my dreams and I think I've got everything sussed. Which is hysterical, really because, well, it's me.

Out of all of my friends, when it comes to relationships I know only one person who has, for the most part, got everything sussed. But I seem to be particularly useless. I meet any halfway pretty girl and part of me instantly knows I am in big trouble. If we were watching me play out any one of my past (please God not future) relationships on a cinema screen, it would look something like this:

I meet a girl. Any girl. This girl seems much, much better than me. Way above my pay grade. Popular, smart, funny, captivating. I believe I am the opposite of all these things. When she smiles, and meets my awkward interest in her with flirtation, I am beside himself. This never happens to me. I simply will not believe that someone like her could see me – really, truly see me and who I really am – and still want to be with me.

We go on a few dates and start down that road together.

I realise pretty quickly that just being myself isn't going to work. On my own, without success, money, powerful friends, status, I am little more than a shadow. I need to pull out *all* the stops early on. Otherwise she'd be out of there in a heartbeat and I wouldn't survive that. So I do. I spend money like there is no tomorrow on presents and holidays and restaurants, all designed to keep her with me. If she isn't working but wants to find a job, I use what connections I have to get her one. I give her money. A lot of money, because I have to compensate her for choosing to be with me. I flatter her. Tell her everything I think she wants to hear. I dedicate my life to anticipating and meeting her every need, even if it is made clear, on occasion with unimaginable cruelty, that I frequently fall short.

I ignore every single red flag (and there are invariably a lot of them) and tell myself that this could be perfect. That I am the one with the problem. Love will fix whatever is wrong. I can make everything better by sheer force of will. That if I try a bit harder surely it will all be OK. I tell everyone else the same thing, making sure no one sees any of the darkness – to the outside world she is perfection and we are both so happy. I just want to be a guy capable of having a relationship. I want to be a Mr and Mrs, a boyfriend and girlfriend, and for the world to see that I am not such a freak show because of it.

But deep down and from very early days I know it isn't right: we shout and scream, and make up and fuck. Constantly. Relentlessly. I try and make her leave. Numerous times. But always end up begging her to come back because I know this is the best I can ever hope for and being alone is intolerable. I am pushed to breaking point, but just at the moment when we are about to split in two, there is a pulling back, a mutual hesitation to actually tip us over the edge, and the moment passes.

There are brief moments of real tenderness and a deep, profound, connected love. Moments where I believe in us, in her, in me. But it grinds us down eventually. I get progressively sicker and sicker, the toll on my/our mental and physical health deteriorating daily. Until there's nothing left of me and I am finished. After years of the same dance, I am all out of life. And, like an unfortunate cancer, there is no chance of remission. Because I know that long-term issues that have been hidden away but never dealt with make long-term relationships – anyterm relationships – impossible, and that the shit always rises eventually.

The relationship ends. The hopeful silver lining is that we will break the cycle, learn lessons, both finally be set free and be able to move on to happier futures. But as the late, great Glenn Gould says, 'behind every silver lining is a cloud' . . .

The End.

Repeat ad infinitum.

This pattern of mad and bad relationships is weighing heavily on me here in Spain. It's because of the 'parking ticket', but also maybe because of what this particular trip is really about.

I've come out to Madrid again because I've been asked to speak at the Save the Children World Congress. Imagine that for a minute – being asked to speak in front of people who are devoting their lives and careers to helping children. People who give of themselves selflessly with no expectation of reward and are met every day with obscene injustices and stories that make my childhood seem picture-perfect. There's no way I could let my boring personal problems get in the way of that.

While I'm here, I'm also going to be filming for a Sunday night Spanish TV show. It's called *Salvados* and is, apparently, a big deal – the Spanish equivalent to *60 Minutes* or *Panorama*. They want to film a concert I am giving in El Escorial and spend a day or two interviewing me for an hour-long documentary. Again, it's going to involve more in-depth conversations about me, music, my past.

I am submerged in sadness from the start of the journey at Heathrow. For this one I am alone. No Denis to wait for (or not) while he goes for a piss or to throw some of my sorrow at or ask to talk me down. I feel half empty and shell-shocked by what's happened with the 'parking ticket' – the council is being hyper-aggressive and vicious, and it's pretty much all I'm bloody thinking about – and to cap it all off I have chosen to speak about what happened to me as a kid to a room full of strangers and to a TV crew.

I feel completely overwhelmed. The fact that I'm going to do this talk and follow it with a bunch of press and then a sold-out concert all in the space of five days is not helping. I think of friends of mine in similar jobs, ones that involve performing, travelling and exposure, and they all seem so goddam adroit at it. Handling the travel, pressure and demands as if it's something they've gently glided into with all the tools necessary to accomplish great things. I feel a stab, not of jealousy, but of intense self-hatred. If they can do this so easily then why am I so shit at it?

It's awful how this job that I've dreamed of for so many decades is threatening to become a chore at times. I feel, and it's something I could never bring myself to admit and so it's just a very faint threat of a feeling, that perhaps I'm losing sight of the magic of the music.

The night before the talk I'm doing a book signing at the largest Fnac in Madrid for the Spanish edition of *Instrumental*. Signings are always a bit weird – people waiting to get a scrawl on a book and maybe a photo. I don't understand the attraction and always assume there'll only be a couple of dozen people there. When I arrive at the Fnac, I find people queuing over four floors, out onto the street and halfway down the block, just to get an autograph. This baffles me. I think perhaps my mind simply cannot allow good stuff like this to make it through its force field unfiltered. Because that would mean trusting in good things. Believing in good things. Expecting good things. My head spins it as some kind of con and is just waiting for me to be exposed to everyone as the imposter I am. Or else it assumes it's all some terrible mistake/joke/coincidence/dumb luck. I also worry that people will get upset waiting for too long and am determined to move things along as quickly as possible, presuming that, like me, everyone is always in a rush.

But they're not in a rush. This is important to them, for reasons only they know. They're also incredibly nice. Some bring gifts, some want hugs, almost all want a photo and I'm there for ages. I hear uplifting stories, and so many people tell me how much this book has helped them. This book that I sweated over for months and then almost killed myself over in an attempt to fight the injunction. I hear these stories and it seems for a moment that the pain, exposure and humiliation were all worthwhile. The mother who came with her brave daughter and who, just the day before the signing, had gone to the police with her to make a statement about her past abuse having got the courage to do so after reading *Instrumental*. The man in his sixties who after finishing the book made an appointment with a therapist for the first time in his life to talk about his past. The girl who was on escorted leave from a psychiatric hospital where they gave her a copy of *Instrumental* and who wanted to have a hug and feel reassured that everything would be OK.

On the one hand I'm wrestling with my own personal grief, the like of which I've never known before (the loss of a marriage, even a flawed one, will do that to a chap), and on the other I'm being met with so much kindness that I feel completely detached from reality. Kindness is the best and the worst thing. I love trying my best to give it, but can't bear to receive it. I suppose I easily mistake it for pity or weakness. But it isn't. It's genuine and replenishing if I can just shut my fucking head up and accept it at face value.

Still, hearing all these stories is intense, beautiful and slightly overwhelming. After the signing I call my shrink several times in tears from my hotel room. He charges me a retainer every month and I get to call him when I'm not so good, and talking to him will, I hope, help. It's all been too much: thinking about my past, preparing for the talk, listening to others tell me about their experiences. Except it's not helping at all. He's an asshole and a bit of a charlatan who always tells me that the cure for PTSD is simply to 'stop it'. Today's gem is when he tells me *Instrumental*, which he's read, is a lie because in that book I give the impression I know how to do certain things and handle certain situations that clearly I'm not able to do. He says I write so well about relationships, that I give the impression I know exactly what it takes to have a happy marriage, but at the end of the day, given my two divorces, it is all clearly bullshit and I'm a fraud. Simultaneously he says that I could end all my unhappiness overnight if I wanted to just by 'stopping it right now'. Which doesn't help my mood. I assume that, because he's the professional and I'm the patient, he's always right even if it feels very wrong. He's also asked me a few times if we could work together, me playing the piano and then interviewing him on stage while he talks about how to fix people's heads. And even I know that's a messed-up thing to suggest.

I need to walk away from this guy. In a couple of weeks, I will. But for now he's one of my few lifelines. Even if it's frustrating and feels fucked up, he's someone to talk to, someone paid to listen. Like a hooker for my head.

The good thing is that I'd anticipated my meltdown. I knew it was going to be a tough few days. So I've made sure that I have time to practise the piano while I'm in Madrid, something that's usually difficult to do when on the road. The TV production team have found me a room with a piano to rehearse on in Teatro Real, the city's opera house. It will give me a rare moment of calm each day I'm there. After my terrible conversation with my shrink I need that. The following morning I wander in, walking past photos of history's finest conductors and singers, and am guided to a ballet rehearsal room which has a decent Yamaha grand and an extraordinary view of Madrid. I sit and play. I lose myself – it's like plugging myself into an emotional electrical outlet. Recharging, renewing, replenishing. The loneliness subsides a little and the sadness changes flavour somewhat. It's less brittle and sharp, more enveloping and even comforting.

When I meet the *Salvados* crew a few hours later at a massive concert hall so that they can interview me, I feel a bit readier, and talk for four hours on camera. We cover childhood, music, trauma, mental health, more music. It is challenging to open up about certain things but I know it's worthwhile. The crew are terrific. I notice that one of the producers is dead pretty and seems particularly attentive towards me. Of course I can't help thinking about what it would be like to explore the city together, find some companionship during the lonely moments, sleep with her. But it doesn't happen. Nothing like that can happen at the moment. I'm too lost, and trying to find answers in the arms of a stranger for a few hours never works for me even if it seems like an easy option. It's another time I find myself jealous of the Tinder crew who seem to be absolutely OK with shagging anything that moves, Buddhist-style (no attachment).

I had, in a moment of abject loneliness, signed up for Tinder a week or so before to see what all the fuss was about.

And regretted it instantly.

I swiped like the wind, moving from 'selective' (liking one girl per hundred, ages 25–35 within 5km) to 'ANYONE PLEASE' (all females everywhere, 18–48 within 50km) within a day, and only got three matches. Two of which were spam. That felt good.

I head back to my hotel post-filming and have a solitary night. I order room service and stare at something HBO on my computer screen, doing all I can not to call the wrong person, not to send a misguided text or email, to try and sit and be still and retain some of my dignity. But tomorrow is the Save the Children talk and I can't settle. Unbelievably, my creepy therapist decides to send me weird, angry texts at midnight, saying things like 'as long as James is right then who cares, eh?' It's such a shock that the anger barely registers. I trust this guy, he's a professional, I can't quite believe he's acting like this. So I medicate myself until I sleep. I just don't want to feel this much. I don't have the tools for it yet.

The next morning I'm up early to prepare for the talk. I'm struggling to find the line between oversharing and staying true to myself. But I remind myself that sometimes, as with the *Guardian* article and the *Salvados* interview, it's worth exposing oneself if it makes a difference. And the fact is that, for some weird reason, I am making a difference. Everywhere I go, I've been inundated with messages of support and gratitude, I've met survivors of abuse and their friends and family who have read *Instrumental* and found some sense of solace and comfort. And here in Spain, I've had politicians called to account on the radio and asked about child protection laws and their ridiculous statute of limitations. *Instrumental* has even been sent to certain prisoners who are incarcerated for child abuse crimes in order to help with their rehabilitation. When I first heard that, I felt physically nauseous. The very idea that the kind of person who did those things to me would now be reading it and, who knows, even getting off on it, was awful and felt like a violation. But I was assured that they chose the offenders very carefully and it was really helping them. Still conflicted about this.

However, at the conference, I try not to take any prisoners. I talk in depth about the fact that in the UK a teacher can walk into a classroom, see another teacher raping a seven-year-old girl, quietly shut the door and carry on with her day without reporting it. And that if she were to do that she would not be committing any crime because the UK is one of the only countries in the world that doesn't have mandatory reporting. It's insane. In the UK, reporting abuse in an institutional setting (schools, hospitals, clerical settings etc.) is entirely discretionary even if someone directly witnesses abuse. There is zero obligation to report anything to anyone. And if someone is brave enough to do so, they have no whistle-blower protection, can be fired, and still there's no legal recourse. Google it if you don't believe me. And then try and avoid punching the wall and weeping in frustration.

I talk about the sort of legacy this kind of abuse leaves. A child who is terrified and who doesn't sleep because they're too scared to and because their head has no off-switch is permanently exhausted. And fear, when coupled with exhaustion, leads to indescribable isolation and a sense of total aloneness. That loneliness is just as damaging as the physical act of abuse.

I talk about incidences of child abuse in 2014–15 being at their highest for a decade and the sad fact that charities like

Save the Children will never not need to exist. That the refugee camps are like a shopping mall for paedophiles and that more, much more, needs to be done to help the most vulnerable. I find myself getting increasingly depressed as I speak about the sheer scale of it all.

I talk about my own experiences because I promised myself years ago that if I were ever lucky enough to be given a platform, no matter how small, I would make sure I used it to talk about things like this. Because fuck you if you think I should shut up. It's so important to talk. It goes against everything we are taught ('If you ever tell anyone . . . don't say a word . . . you'd better keep our secret') and it is the most uncomfortable thing in the world to do. I turn red, can't make eye contact, lower my voice, try and become small and invisible when describing what I've been through. Yet talking is the only possible way through. For people who have been through severe emotional trauma, not talking about it is the equivalent of a diabetic not taking insulin. It can and will kill you.

I know it can seem indulgent. I know it can come across as victimy and whiny. I berate myself enough for those things as it is. But there is simply no other choice. It's talk or die. They say time heals all wounds but that is a fucking lie. Time does not heal these wounds, and anyone who claims otherwise is in a boatload of denial. I'll never forgive, I'll never forget and I'll always be angrier than hell about it. But while I'm still here I ain't going to shut up about it. It's my experience, it belongs to me. It broke me physically and emotionally. It almost cost me everything. And it's taken me decades to put things back together again in some semblance of order. It hasn't defined who I am but it has certainly forged certain parts of me that are skewed, faulty and messy.

I end with a call to action. I make it clear that, although perhaps the CEO of Save the Children is notionally the most important person in the room that day, in truth, the person sitting in each and every seat is the most important person: everyone in the room that day has a vital part to play in making a difference. I am in awe of every single one of them.

But even though I've opened up somewhat, the things I say are diluted to the point of vapour. Of course they are. The speech I'd really want to give feels impossible.

(Trigger warning here, so feel free to skip the next two paragraphs if you're feeling fragile).

If I was brave, then I'd show them all a picture of me as a six-year-old. I was skinny. Tiny. Beautiful. Or as certain types of people would say, hot as fuck. I weighed less than 50lbs. He was 6 foot tall and weighed maybe 220. I hadn't seen a dick before other than my own tiny thing, but his looks enormous. It is terrifying and red and veiny and hairy and it smells bad. Imagine being pinned face down, head pushed and held down onto the floor while something that big is forced into something so small. Can you even begin to contemplate the physics involved in that act? The force that would have to be applied and the physical damage that would result? Can you try and conceive of the extreme physical pain of that experience? And then see yourself being pulled up and flung onto your knees like a rag doll, being punched and slapped and having it forced into your mouth and not being able to breathe, choking and thinking 'I'm going to die now' and then feeling like you're drowning. Imagine believing in your core self that this is happening because of something you have done. There is no one to talk about it with. There is no way out. Life carries on around you in colour while you walk around in black and white pretending you are a part of it all.

Imagine this happening for years. It being allowed to continue. Protecting the man who did this by maintaining your silence and acting normally when you are around other people and he is there. Cleaning blood off your legs alone in a locked bathroom. Wiping away stray pieces of shit from your thighs. Gagging at the smell. Hiding all of it from everyone all the time. Pissing yourself regularly. Dealing with a lifetime of intestinal and groin issues. Having metal rods in your back where doctors tried to fix the damage as a constant reminder of how shameful you are.

The vast majority of people won't experience things like that, thank God. But I'm also aware the vast majority would rather just talk about 'child abuse' as a generic, vague concept and then acknowledge how awful it is. I want, no I *need* them, to get as close to the experience of it as possible because otherwise it remains sanitised, hypothetical, a million times prettier than the reality. I'd say thank you to everyone in that room who has dedicated their lives to helping victims of abuse. But then that kid inside me would say 'fuck you' as well. Because they *have* to work harder, try harder, not rest and not stop until more has been done. They have barely scratched the surface, and while we continue to insulate ourselves from the horror of it all it is continuing to happen on a scale that is unimaginable.

I'd say to them that yes, perhaps it looks like I've come out the other side. I have a successful career, seem to have got my shit together. But I also have arms covered in scars, a shiny assortment of mental health diagnoses, months of inpatient psych ward experience, multiple suicide attempts. I've experienced a hundred different medications, and most days I have the urge to eviscerate myself. I haven't truly come out of anything and I feel like I'm on borrowed time, and while we're all sitting here in this big fancy auditorium being served coffee and pastries there are hundreds of thousands of children going through what I went through and worse every single second of every single day, and why aren't we all doing more, much, much more?

But I don't say any of that. Because I don't know what would happen to my mind if I did.

After the talk I'm feeling exposed and vulnerable. I walk and walk, smoke and drink coffee, inhale the city and repeat my little stroking phrases to myself, out loud and in my head. I feel so much pain I even go to Starbucks for a coffee in a desperate attempt at distracting myself.

In Madrid.

Starbucks.

Ordering a grande fucking cappuccino.

Later, back at my hotel for the night, I lock the door, switch off my phone and try really hard to calm down by using the cat-and-mouse method. I find myself attempting to reach beyond and behind the chatter in my mind and simply sit with this sadness I'm feeling. It is so much harder for me to do this while alone. In front of a camera with a TV crew, on stage in front of an audience or in front of a date there are always distractions and ways to shove the feelings back down to avoid feeling truly insane. When it's just me I'm completely undiluted and it's scary. I want to be able simply to witness my feelings. Just watch and wait, and see them for what they are: an entirely appropriate reaction to current life events. It's so difficult to do that. It's the mental equivalent of sitting in a café alone and not looking at your phone. Just sitting there, alone with your thoughts while everyone else thinks you're some kind of psychopath.

It doesn't work. Somehow I make it through the night. I can't figure out how I ended up the other side of the maze safe and sound and in one piece when all I wanted to do was jump out of the window, but I do. There are moments of peace, I drift in and out of sleep, time passes without my realising and, before I know it, I'm waking up to sunlight and birds and that habitual early-morning feeling of slight confusion and sadness – nothing specific, just a flavour of a memory lingering at the back of my mind that isn't catastrophic but feels slightly ominous. A sustained D minor chord loitering like a shark underneath a major-key nursery rhyme.

El Escorial is an hour outside of Madrid, a place where all the rich people go to chill out when they need to escape the city. Home to one of the largest monasteries in the world, it's a breathtakingly beautiful town, from what I can see from the car window. I make an attempt to explore it after I've checked into my hotel. I walk for ten minutes, look at the monastery from the outside, inhale the spirituality emanating from it, freak out at being around so many people and then scurry back to my room where I spend five hours watching Danish crime drama.

Whatever glimmers of stillness I'd felt the previous evening were clearly fleeting and have by now completely evaporated. I am still grieving my marriage, still feel like I'm serving a prison sentence for a crime I may not have even committed, still teetering on the edge of some kind of mental precipice. I know I need to get my head into gear for the concert this evening but I just can't. It has run away with itself again. And I've no distractions, no means of escape, just a dark, small hotel room and the voices in my head telling me I'm crap at everything.

The soundcheck goes well enough. But the concert itself isn't my best. The hall is completely rammed, with 1,200 people in it, and I'm wracked with fear, especially because the *Salvados* crew are filming it. From my perspective, there are too many fluffed notes, my head is too distracted by 'parking tickets' and past traumas, and even the music I'm playing can't defeat those voices that night. I feel that all in all I could have played so much better. Except for one piece.

Chopin's F minor *Fantasie*.

I am proud of that one. It's a good performance. The interpretation is what I wanted. The sound is what I wanted. I managed to hit every ridiculous octave jump, where both hands are stretched as wide as they can while moving rapidly up and down the keyboard in opposite directions, each hand manoeuvring in slightly different ways and negotiating marginally different distances to the other one. There are a bunch of them and they almost always trip me up in live performance. I even nail the awkward descending run in chromatic sixths on the last page (fellow pianists will appreciate this even if no one else does), and feel solid at the keyboard throughout the piece – still, strong, no shakes, fingers buried deep inside the keys.

While I was on stage playing it, time really did disappear. I felt a bit like I did when I was eighteen and took acid while listening to Glenn Gould playing the Goldberg Variations – back then I saw Gould right there in front of me jumping on the notes of a giant piano in time with the music, everything in slow motion. Now it's not quite as trippy, but there's definitely a sense of other-worldliness. Of being detached from my own miserable reality and connected to something greater. And that, right there, is the magic. That's why I do this job – to somehow reach back through time and fully connect with and inhabit a 200-year-old composition is an astonishing feeling. In an instant I am less alone and more a part of something good where everything is possible, inspiring, friendly and worthy. Something infinitely more important than me and my uninspired, ridiculous problems. The 'parking ticket' is forgotten, the need for distraction and escape leaves me and I'm just there, floating on stage and present. For those fourteen minutes my head is blissfully quiet.

But when the gig ends I'm panicking because so many simple things that were fine in rehearsal didn't come off in some of the other pieces. I'm also worried that the *Salvados* crew will use the shit bits of the concert in the TV show rather than the good bits. I've managed to convince myself the post-gig signing will be a disaster and that people will feel so disappointed they'll just want to leave. Truth is, I get taken into the lobby after walking offstage, and it seems like all 1,200 people are there waiting for a book to be signed, a photo to be taken, a CD to be dedicated. It's ridiculous. Even the staff all stay behind and ask for a group photo a couple of hours later. And right at that moment I think: even if it wasn't my best gig, who fucking cares? Am I the only one who feels that unless something is perfect (a girlfriend, wife, job, gig, car, restaurant, movie, whatever) it's a disaster? If nothing else, I can guarantee that at least one person in that hall that night heard something new and extraordinary and went away feeling better about their life. And that's got to be worth celebrating.

There's something else that's potentially worth celebrating. That evening I get a text. It's from an actress I met a few weeks ago. She's twenty-seven. Fourteen years younger than me. Shut up. She wants to meet up. It's my first date in for ever and I want it to count, to be sure I'm not just starting something for the wrong reasons. For me as well as her. So I get tickets for the opera back in London for a few days after I get home.

It's my favourite one in the world (*Così fan tutte*, about which more later) and she's never been to the opera before and has always wanted to. This seems like the perfect introduction, and it's at the Covent Garden Opera House, which is *so beautiful*. I pull some strings and manage to get a table in the conservatory at the most romantic restaurant in London which is a one-minute walk from the venue. (Clos Maggiore – go. Please go. It's so romantic that even just a coffee there might very well have saved at least one of my marriages.) We'll have dinner there after the performance. It looks, on paper, to be the perfect night.

It turns out that it comes pretty damn close to perfect. The actress looks stunning, the music is sublime, the staging immaculate and thrilling and three hours pass in no time. At 10.15 p.m. we wander slowly, arm in arm, to the restaurant. They've seated us directly under the most extraordinary flowers and plants in the corner of the conservatory. It's the most beautiful room I've ever seen: warm, colourful, intimate, luxurious, filled with the scent of flowers and candles. I've brought her a little necklace with a mandala (an Indian spiritual symbol of the universe) because I know she likes shit like that. And, if I'm honest, I feel the same way. Even if I pretend to be gruff and cynical sometimes, the right kind of spiritual stuff moves me to tears worryingly often.

The food is outta this world. The service spectacular. It's all so *right*. The best thing is that we definitely seem to have a connection. She says kind things to me, we laugh a lot. She makes me feel good about myself.

A couple of hours later (yep, two hours for dinner; a record for me), we're in a cab heading back to mine where we stay up until 4 a.m. talking, fucking, dancing, listening to music. She's much more street than I am. She introduces me to some spectacular songs. I'm constantly amazed, and a bit embarrassed, at how little I know about other genres of music. Most people my age know all this other stuff that's out there – it's not that I don't like it or don't want to get to know it, more I don't really feel the need to explore other things. As a kid I had perhaps a slightly eclectic taste in music – Queen, Bucks Fizz (I'm sorry), Wham! (not sorry – the first autobiography I ever read was George Michael's), Bach, Michael Jackson, Bon Jovi

(*Slippery When Wet* saved my ass), Beethoven. But now I listen almost exclusively to classical. I figure that the whole classical repertoire would take me several hundred years to really get to grips with and that's more than enough for me. But then I meet someone like this woman and somehow I'm learning about astonishing new music (God bless Spotify) after having sat in a restaurant for two whole hours eating dinner.

The next morning, we wake up drowsy and groggy, late, and wander down the road for brunch somewhere achingly trendy, filled with parents of kids called Hercules and Lion, but it's all good because I feel great, she's still pretty, it wasn't an illusion and, most surprising of all to me, she really seems to like me. Even though I'm so much older than her. And a bit of a mess. And clearly not good enough for her. Perhaps this is another one of those times that my head has been telling me half-truths and outright lies which have been, temporarily at least, contradicted by reality.

Weirdly she is even OK with my squeaks and tics. One of the legacies of a difficult past is that the pain sometimes comes out sideways, especially if it hasn't been properly verbalised at the time. I have to squeak at a certain pitch, cough in a certain way, touch things, tap things and so on. It's kind of like Tourette's (diagnosis no. 14 for me) and makes life challenging at times (especially mid-concert or mid-date). Usually on a date I do all I can to keep them in. Which is awful because they have to come out somehow, so if they don't come out through my mouth I start squirming in my seat or on the bed, my shoulder or head having to touch whatever it's lying on in a certain way, my wrist having to flex a certain way. I either look like I've got ants crawling over parts of me or like someone who's having a stroke. Occasionally I just can't help squeaking out my little Tourette's anthem, but when that happens this girl just smiles and thinks it's 'cute'.

She really liked *Rain Man*.

I know it's unlikely to last. I want to have a deep, fulfilling, healthy(ish) long-term relationship in time. But I'm not going to be ready for that for a while, and whoever I end up going down that road with will deserve to have me vaguely shipshape for it. Which means not diving straight into something now. At most I'm capable of a summer fling for a couple of months. And the good thing is that I haven't done my usual thing of promising the world while knowing I can't give even a tiny village. I've been very open and honest with her about what I am and am not able to handle at the moment. She seems fine with that. Which feels liberating. This idea that I can tell the truth and someone will still want to be with me is astounding to me.

The actress is helping to raise my self-esteem a notch. Truth is, if I hadn't met her and started whatever it was we started, I don't think I'd have survived the 'parking ticket' and the countless sleepless nights of worry, rage, grief and distress. While I know genuine peace of mind needs to come from inside me, I'm lazy and will invariably opt for the illusory easier, softer way. I'm happy to let this fling try and shoulder the responsibility for a while.

Don't pretend for a *minute* you'd act any differently.

AFFIRMATION 3:

'I let go and allow the universe
to gently hold and support me.
I am never given more than I
can handle!'

TRANSLATION:

'HEY, ASSHOLE! CONTROLLING THINGS KEEPS US ALL SAFE.
DON'T YOU DARE EVEN THINK ABOUT LETTING GO.'

Chopin *Polonaise-fantasie*

The *Polonaise-fantasie* is last Chopin, not late Chopin. The last full-scale piano work he composed before he died aged thirty-nine. The more I study it, inhabit it and play it, the more I realise it's his greatest achievement (with the possible exception of the fourth Ballade). Chopin was so broken after the end of his relationship with George Sand that he had nowhere else to put it other than in his music. He had realised by this stage of his life that people were living in their own heads, distracted all the time and unable to really listen. Yep. Even back in the 1840s we were constantly distracted assholes. And rather than accept that and let people talk and smooch and cough through his concerts (concerts is perhaps too grand a word as he loathed giving them; instead he'd play to small groups of people, usually by candlelight, in his living room), he uses music as the vehicle to demand our attention and, as the great pianist Jeremy Denk writes in his blog *Chopin for Dummies*, weaves the act of listening into the very fabric of this piece.

We all need to learn to listen more. In particular, to ourselves. It's a dying art. We have forgotten how to shut the fuck up. We have conversations with people who tell us they're listening but while we're speaking all they're really doing is reloading, ready to fire off another salvo of words as soon as we shut up. We distract ourselves constantly with inane chatter both real and imagined. We occasionally, usually by mistake, end up spending time alone with our thoughts and then scream and run as fast and as far as possible. And this is why I love classical music so much – for me it's the delivery agent to the soul. It has very long, complex pieces, but for a reason; it goes deep inside, to our very core, and that complexity resonates there and improves things at that deeper level.

In this piece, we get these extraordinary moments of aural slaps around the face – repeated chords, weird harmonies, sudden U-turns in pace or volume, bizarre harmonic shifts. Chopin is forcing us to listen. And when we do we are rewarded with something completely extraordinary. It's like inhabiting a dream that you don't want to wake up from. Some of his most personal thoughts and feelings are hidden away in there for us to absorb and experience.

It's no surprise that it's a lonely piece, a sad piece. It contains some of his most poignant and beautiful melodies, some of his most intimate, private moments. Even the ending, usually heroic and virtuosic in a big solo piano composition (the musical equivalent of buying a Porsche when you turn fifty), fades away and dissipates as he fuses two endings into one – the heroic one and the sad one merged together, a fucked-up hybrid. Like he's ending a thought and not a piece of music. The whole thing doesn't really have a defined structure per se, but it is tightly controlled and concentrated. There is not a single note too many and not one too few. There are times when he threatens to let go (halfway through there are some monstrous chromatics and really gnarly chords where the train almost comes hurtling off the tracks) but at the last minute he bails and reins it in almost as if he's scared of what will happen if he really does let go. It's an awkward, scary mixture of freeform improvisation and intense control all at once (or dating, as I call it). He's in his brain-dungeon, scrabbling against the cell walls with his fingers, trying to tunnel through the bricks into the sunlight and bleeding with the effort.

*

LONDON, SEPTEMBER 2016

It's concert day again, and just like in Madrid last month, I wake up and know instantly that something is very wrong. It's 4 a.m. I am, quite suddenly and seemingly without warning, enveloped with terror. All the voices inside me are so loud and so raucous that they're not even screaming words at me, it's just a wall of noise.

It feels like I have a living, breathing monster inside me. When this happens I sometimes get scared it's going to strangle me. Just full-on fucking asphyxiate me. Invariably, it'll happen on days I'm going to have to perform, but it'll also assault me while walking to a café, sitting in the cinema or waiting on a tube platform. But I've not had this happen so frequently for several years.

My biggest fear is of it happening on stage, mid-performance, the panic and terror taking over and breaking me in two. Music – the great, consistent love of my life – finally letting me down and finishing me off, the one thing I've always trusted being the catalyst for my own destruction.

The pressure and responsibility of walking on stage, doing something that has been so profoundly important and so literally life-saving to me, feels at times so immense that it could spill over into a full-on breakdown at any point. Luckily it hasn't happened yet, but it haunts me, God it haunts me.

I know this may come across as precious and pretentious and 'artistic'. It's not. It's just that I've devoted my entire life to the very thing that saved it – music. And the fact that this miracle cure, the only reason I'm still alive, could turn on me even more viciously than angry ex-wives or meds that used to make you feel safe and now suddenly make you want to set fire to yourself is terrifying. My entire world would simply collapse were that ever to happen.

I shuffle through to the kitchen in my boxer shorts, hairy, spindly, paper-white legs on display, arms like cotton buds poking out of my too-big, ill-fitting T-shirt. I feel the panic rising as the reality kicks in that the concert is in sixteen hours and I've woken up with this noise inside me, my head ablaze and no way of quelling it. Picturing myself just sitting there on stage like a giant slab of peeled back muscle, mucus and caustic fucking flesh. The thousands and thousands of notes all lost and swirling and untamed like butterflies, with me, a retarded mental patient, chasing after them with a net.

I'm terrified I'm going to mess up. A giant memory lapse. Fistfuls of wrong notes. Having to stop. Dying.

This is when my OCD is unleashed. My psyche has pulled the emergency alarm and it is sending in troops to try and help control the situation. Mental martial law. It starts with an immediate and alarming increase in tapping and squeaking, switching lights on and off. I wash my hands repeatedly and line up all my things in the right way. I try making lists to attempt to control my mind, and of course it doesn't really work because by this stage it is unstoppable in its overwhelm. The next few hours will involve a maelstrom of taxis booked, scores pored over, complimentary tickets confirmed, piano practised, pasta eaten, anecdotes and dates and one-liners memorised and rehearsed, scores pored over again, the pieces having to be played through in the mind perfectly again and again, jumping in at odd moments to check memory, right *there* in the middle of a phrase or a bar, trying to trip me up, knowing it would, taking immense satisfaction in the jolt of fear that occurs when it does, iPhone Scrabble game started and played again and again until I'm winning (it's only safe to turn it off if I'm scoring at least thirty-seven more points than the computer), keys, cards and cash lined up in the right way, calendar checked again and again and again, the day is right, the time is right, it is happening, it's OK, it's not OK, medicine taken, dosages measured out and dispensed and planned with military precision even if it often results in friendly fire, tea drunk, cigarettes allotted, plotted and pined for, one each ninety minutes, scores pored over yet again, satchel packed, checked, rechecked, checked, rechecked, checked, repacked, rechecked, lights switched on and off the correct number of times, multiple alarms set for pills, meditation, cigarettes, food and cabs, arms and tendons gently stretched, clothes laid out, scores left on the piano because I don't need them any more, scores collected because actually I do need them, I don't need them, I do need them, if I bring them with me I won't need them, if I leave them I will need them, but then if that's true everything else I do to keep myself safe counts and the pressure to do all of those special things correctly is unsustainable, I just, please God, want it all to stop.

This piss-stream of consciousness.

Just for a minute.

The relief of it stopping would be nirvana.

It's only half past five in the morning. I'm already exhausted. Which means I'm going to get ill. I'm already ill (hello hypochondria, my old friend!). My immune system is so fucking weak because I'm so fucking weak. A pussy little bitch. I'll bray in a whiny insufferable voice about my HUGE AND IMPORTANT CONCERT that's coming up but handle it like a sickly runt. A runt cunt.

I don't think I'm going to be able to do it. Not cheaply at any rate. I write cheques with my mouth that my mind can't cash. I do it every day, a thousand times over.

'I'm a concert pianist,' I smug at people.

'I will do that concert,' I self-import at my manager.

And then the day comes and the cost is a thousand times the fee I'm getting paid. I'm in the most expensive club in the world – the membership fee alone for being made like me is extortionate. Do you ever feel like that? I'm pretty sure it's common enough. The club may be expensive but I don't think it's that exclusive. Toxic levels of shame, terror, paranoia and despair flood through my system at every available opportunity.

I am in emotional and mental debt up to my eyeballs, the bail-iffs constantly trying to beat down the door. And once again, if I am this on-the-floor exhausted now, how the hell am I going to make it through to tonight and perform for a hundred, a thousand, twenty, any number of people?

I'm letting them down. All of them. I'm used to doing this at concerts by now, the big ones and the small ones. Me, I let down all the time. Fuck it. But the audience? My best friend who's coming? The girl I like? The guy from *The Times*? My mum? The lighting guy? And worst of all, the composers whose memories I am shitting all over. Chopin. Bach. Beethoven. My holy trinity. With my spastic, galumphing hands, Swiss-cheese memory, faux-self-deprecating bow and stench of neediness. They would be disgusted.

I force myself back into the present moment and focus on the mundane, the practicalities. Like breakfast.

I always make porridge on Concert Day if I'm at home. Another pointless control thing that I imbue with magical, mystical qualities. I weigh out 40 grams of porridge, 200ml of milk. Shove the lot in a saucepan and turn on the hob. I've been in relationships where it seemed that if I didn't eat enough, they would leave me. Well, not leave me. Chuck me out. For 'not taking care of myself'. The message is basically, 'Be a fucking man, eat a lot, definitely eat more than me, be strong and a good hunter-gatherer and make me feel safe and protected like a princess. Otherwise I'll find someone else who will.'

So I eat. Make a pretence of wanting to get big and strong. Which I actually do want. But while in principle I really like the idea of being tough, healthy and therefore attractive, I don't see it as truly viable. I know it'll never happen. Imagine the effort required to accomplish that: weights, protein powder, jogging, crunches, protein-tracking apps, gym memberships, protein bars, talking about gym memberships, being a cunt. Impossible. I've too much agonising to do.

I sit on the sofa with my bowl and start eating. I just need to finish it quickly, take a shit (it's already bubbling up inside my guts and starting to hurt), and get to my piano. I force it down, not tasting it, not hungry, just needing fuel, impatient inpatient.

I wash my bowl meticulously, dry it well and place it carefully on top of the two other bowls in my possession, even though I'm dying to go to the loo. There's a faint sheen of sweat on my face. It's getting progressively worse, starting to drip as the pain in my stomach intensifies. I need it to come out but I'm not sure which end it'll come out of. I'm sat there on the toilet trying to breathe, counting out loud to try and calm myself down, my head getting hot and tingling, a towel pressed against my forehead, something alive and bad crawling over my skin, trying to think of other things, nicer things, happier times, and just when I think I'm going to pass out, the lower half of my body falls out of itself, messily, and I feel myself crying with relief and something else, darker, that I can't identify.

It's 6.14 a.m. Here we are again. I don't think it should be this hard. I don't think anything should be this hard. I have to force my legs into doing what they should be able to do naturally, even though it feels like trudging through quicksand, and walk into the bedroom to get dressed.

I shuffle into my office. The office is a tiny room at the back of my flat. It has a small upright piano and nothing else of any importance. It's my safe place where I can hide. I fall through the door and collapse onto the piano stool. I realise I've another thirteen hours of this before I'll be on stage, and it feels unsustainable. I'm exhausted. Beyond exhausted. I can't rest and I can't stop. I force myself to start slowly playing through the pieces I'll be playing later on. It's the best way to check memory. But my head is so noisy I can't focus, I don't pay attention and I find myself finishing several pieces with no recollection of playing them.

Which is a total waste of time because I can't do that on stage; I can't just show up, switch to autopilot and hope for the best. I need to be present at the piano. It's the best thing and the worst thing, but I have to be there.

That means staying in my body while on stage and not giving into any anxiety attacks, listening to myself play, experiencing the music and being visible and focused and able to offer it all out to the audience.

I know how retarded that sounds. I'm not a nuclear physicist or a soldier or a teacher. Perhaps I don't have a job that is, compared to those people, in any real way important, but here's the thing: playing the piano feels for me much the same as someone who has chosen to be a priest feels. Except my faith is in something that actually works. It's really a calling. And it's the only calling I've ever had, so I *can't* fuck it up because if I do then I've got nothing left. It is irreplaceable, it doesn't judge me, talk back or hurt me; it is just there, ready to work its magic.

I slap myself around the face to wake myself up and try and shut the voices of insecurity up. But it's not working. There's just too much noise, fear, motion, emotion, disappointment. It's barely 7 a.m. and my day is ruined.

I take myself to bed. I lie back down in the hope that a couple of hours' rest will reset things.

I sleep three hours – a godsend. I start practising again. I feel way more confident. Either my team of mental hitmen are still asleep, or I've managed to convince some of the happier voices to come out to play.

The concert isn't a grand event at a famous hall. But every gig is equally important. A calling, remember? This one is at a grammar school in Canterbury which is doing superb things for music. They have a thriving music department, a small but carefully allocated budget, great teachers, space and time in the curriculum to study all aspect of music, give numerous concerts and make school trips to music venues. They even have their own music festival, of which my event is the closing concert. I have to get my shit together for it.

I'm pathetically grateful once again for just how often work engagements save my ass at the last minute, even though the run-up is always so painful.

Before I know it it's time to head into town to the station to get my train. I buy my coffee, settle into my seat, listen to Lana Del Rey (the actress put me on to her) and Vladimir Horowitz (separately, not a duet), do the crossword. After a rocky start this day is going a little better. I'm met at Canterbury station, driven to the venue where there's a shitty old grand piano that sounds like death. But I don't care because it's all they've got and it's a school with very little money. Why not make the best of it?

Whoa. Mr Optimistic bounding out of the gates and hitting me right between the eyes.

The kids are amazing – fifteen, sixteen, way more sorted than I could ever have hoped to be at that age, big fans of music and, oddly, me. They'd seen some of the TV shows I'd made, enjoyed a bunch of YouTube videos and listened to me on Spotify and were excited. We take selfies and I rehearse and sneak cheeky smokes round the back of the music building just like the good old days.

They've asked me to give a speech as well as play and so I talk about how impressive this school is compared to the vast majority where music simply doesn't happen. It's devastating to me that although we all know how incredibly important and life-affirming music is, so often it becomes lost, buried under a mountain of red tape and Ofsted inspections and money worries, a luxury rather than a priority. These guys have got it spot on. Music is thriving; the students are thriving. (Politicians, please notice the connection here, you fucking idiots.) There's an orchestra and choirs. Music is running throughout the fabric of the entire school, just as it should be.

I play the *Polonaise-fantasie* by Chopin and the Bach-Busoni Chaconne. The piano feels like it's going to break but somehow holds up, and there's a lot of celebration afterwards. I feel so much pride for these kids who are preparing for A levels and university in an age of what I imagine to be intolerable pressure from every side. What I would give to have that time again, knowing what I know now. How differently things would turn out. Perhaps.

I think I'd say 'fuck you' to people a whole lot more. I'd

remind myself that if I'm lucky enough to have a giant passion for something then I need to not only run with it, I need to run through anything to pursue it and run over/away from anyone who even threatens to get in the way of it. Focus as if my very life depends on it and don't stop. Enjoy that singleness of purpose. Relish it and celebrate it. Don't do it apologetically. Don't take prisoners. Don't hold back. Ignore those people, and there will be many, who don't or won't support and encourage me.

I'd also realise that the fragile, vulnerable part of me I'd tried so hard to hide is actually the part that needs to be explored, developed, nurtured and celebrated more than ever. Handwriting comes below all of this. Ditto algebra. And sport can go fuck itself if you're not built for it and don't enjoy it. And girls aren't as scary as they seem. And it doesn't matter if you say the wrong thing or can't spell certain words or feel too terrified to speak to new people or even, on occasion, speak at all. Fundamentally all is OK because even if they're really good at pretending otherwise, everyone around you has the same fears and the same priorities as you – to be well, to find peace, to love and to be loved. We are all united in our perfectly flawed humanity even if we won't know this for a long time to come.

I'd remind myself constantly that sensitive kids are the absolute best. That it's more often than not the 'weird' kids at school who people most want to hang out with as adults. That sensitivity and gentleness are things to aspire to, not run away from. Children who have a sense of justice, of right and wrong, of empathy and horror at the inhumanity of the world in which we live are the ones who will make generation-impacting changes. Rather than the sporty, uber-popular, cool-as-fuck, shagging-everything-that-moves teenagers that everyone wanted to be when I was at school.

I was a cowardly child. Terrified of attention yet craving it at the same time. Needy and incapable of feeling solid, safe and good enough. We live in the age of the extrovert. To be an extrovert is to be celebrated and rewarded: we poke strangers on Facebook, start arguments on Twitter, take endless selfies, shout photos of ourselves all over the internet. I'd make damn sure, if I had my time over again, that I did whatever it took to celebrate quietness, to make feeling good enough about who I am, irrespective of all the external shit, my number one priority. I'd remind myself that having a million followers on social media is as valid and real as being a millionaire in a game of Monopoly.

The Canterbury kids seem to have nailed all of this. It floors me. I am astonished by teenagers today; they have such an unfair reputation (hoodies, ADHD, gangs, porn, dick pics, entitlement) and yet they seem to be self-assured, polite, charming, humble. All the things I wasn't. I envy them a bit and am in awe of them a lot for it.

I mull all this over on the train back to London. I'm angry. I feel as if I have missed out on my entire childhood and, with it, the chance to be one of those kids I so admire. Maybe, just maybe, with a different set of cards dealt to me I would have turned into an adult I could admire rather than the imitation I see in the mirror. Or not. There's a good chance I could have had a Utopian childhood and still ended up an angry freak. Anger turned inwards is devastatingly toxic and destructive. As is a lack of self-confidence. I wish I could let myself off the hook a little bit.

It does feel like a lost cause, though. Comparable to wanting to grow an arm back by sheer force of will when it's already been amputated after being hit by a drunk driver. And being so furious at your missing arm that you want to lay waste and murder entire civilisations. Rather than blaming the driver you blame yourself for walking down the road that night. You call yourself every name under the sun, verbally, physically, emotionally assault yourself and constantly castigate, belittle, berate and harm yourself, and all for simply being in the wrong place at the wrong time. You do it so often and with such skill and panache that it becomes embedded at a cellular level into the very depths of your soul until it's an unquestioned part of you. But it desperately needs to be questioned. And challenged. And, hopefully, with endless patience and time and compassion, changed.

I get home and into bed and feel unsettled. Sleep doesn't come for ages. So I smoke and listen to talk radio and audio books (I have an Olympic gold in this) until I pass out just as the sun starts to rise.

I'm back in Madrid. It's still September. Still hot. I've been invited to do a TEDx talk about trust. Which makes me fall about laughing given my near total inability to trust anything at all. But I say yes because, honestly, any opportunity to go visit Madrid, even though I never seem to be able to sleep there.

The day before I travel I'm at the House of Lords meeting with around twenty people from music hubs, government, the Arts Council and so on to discuss the state of music education. The one thing we can all agree on, the only thing really, is that music education in the UK is an absolute disaster. We've ended up in a position after years and years of errors and omissions and zero prioritising where the vast majority of state-educated children do not have the opportunity to learn an instrument. The Canterbury grammar school was very much an exception. And nobody seems to know what to do about it. Seeing all these people gathered together, realising yet again that nothing will come of it despite good intentions, is thoroughly depressing.

It plays right into the talk I have to give about trust. Music is the one trustworthy thing that there is and we're taking it away from an entire generation of children. It unites us more than any other art form. Perhaps that's why we all believe in it so much – we can't trust our heads, the voices inside us, even our hearts. But music? No problem. It doesn't ever let us down. We speak that language fluently from birth, the one part of us that life doesn't and can't ruin for us or beat out of us because it forms part of our interior selves. Remember, again, there is nothing more universal than music.

All the more shameful that music is being eradicated from our schools at a rate of knots when it could be fixed so easily, so quickly, by a willing government.

I plan to pour all of this out in Madrid. I'm feeling good about this one, I think because I'm going to be talking about issues close to my heart but without getting too heavy and personal. Also Denis is with me on this trip. We go to soundcheck the evening before the event and there's a moment where I have a wobble, because I'm told that while I talk I'll need to stay still within a big red circle that's been painted on the floor like a giant target. That does my head in because I *have* to pace when I talk. I always pace. I can't answer the phone sitting down, can't hold a conversation without walking around like a caged animal. But Denis reassures me, and suggests I try out the piano on stage instead. It is terrific and it calms me down; suddenly it all feels doable (Denis knows me so well).

The two of us grab an early dinner (we try four places before finding a restaurant that agrees to serve us at 7.45 p.m., and where there is not a single soul there other than us two bums), we talk shop and grab our customary *helado*, which has become a bit of a tradition, and then I head back to go and sleep.

Remarkably, I have a good night (yay, Madrid!). The talk is scheduled for 11 a.m. Which is perfect for me. Less time to lose my shit. I still, just in case, have to go through my little rituals to try and ensure a smooth ride. The 'parking ticket' is still rattling around and trying to set fire to my brain.

I have one last cigarette forty-five minutes before going on stage. God, it tastes good. Never as good as the one immediately after the gig. But almost. It tastes of hope and love and possible redemption.

While I walk up and down anxiously in the wings, I use my hands to do a weird little brushing down of my clothes. It gets rid of negative, stale nervous energy around my arms and torso, and disperses into the atmosphere where it remains off the stage. That's what I tell myself anyway.

The venue, an old slaughterhouse, is rammed. I walk on stage and sit at the piano. There's a hair on the E above middle C that

I have to brush off (or people will die). Then I play the little, miraculous Bach prelude. Tell everyone in the room that they too could be playing that piece within six weeks if they were able to find forty-five minutes a day and focus (and perhaps that I have a new book out soon showing them how to do it). I chat about trust, music, interiority, and then talk about how I'd love to create an app (because we definitely need more apps in the world) that celebrates introverts. The idea would be that every day it would choose a piece of classical music for you, give you some information and context about it and you would then find a few minutes to sit quietly and listen to it. Perhaps share it with someone you loved or were thinking about. And that if you did this every day, just took a few minutes to disappear and go inside yourself, it could radically alter the way you perceive the world.

I then get all the lights to switch off, save for one on the keyboard of the piano, and I ask them to practise now. To close their eyes and truly listen to the piece I'm about to play. To see what happens when they quieten the mind and disappear, notice where the music takes them, trust that all will be well and use this time to stop thinking and just notice and celebrate the miracle that they are – hear themselves breathing, feel their heart beating, experience the feelings that arise, allow their minds to go wherever they want as the music plays. I ask them to commit to doing something like this every day.

I play them this beautiful, slow, gentle piece of music by Gluck from his opera *Orfeo ed Euridice*. For me, it's the ultimate love song. It's the melody that accompanies Orfeo as he descends into the underworld to find and rescue the love of his life. He has no idea if he'll find her, if he'll survive, but love makes us all do stupid shit. It's in D minor, bleak, terribly sad, a musical ode to lost love and shattered dreams. And yet.

And yet . . .

This is the magic trick with classical music: underneath that sadness is an immense pool of surrender, hope, love, even joy. It's like musical sleight of hand. Somehow the gentleness of the melodies, the movement of the harmonies, the simplicity of the piece gives the sadness a flavour of happy. Even the difficult, painful feelings are beautiful in classical music. The sorrow resonates deep inside us and turns, somehow, miraculously, into its opposite.

Everything has gone totally quiet. It's like time has slowed right down and the external world has disappeared. It feels good. Great, even. Imagine this for a minute. What it feels like to be sat at a giant piano. Tuned to perfection. The touch and weight of the keys exactly what you'd hope for. There is total darkness all around you and just a spotlight illuminating the keys. Every note sounds as if it's been hand polished and then released into the ether, twinkling like some beautiful, D minor star. In between the notes there is a silence so deep that it is all-consuming.

The only people in the universe at that moment are you and Gluck. You guys are having a walk together, an exchange that is going beyond words and across time. You hear answers to things you were desperately in need of finding solutions to, and as the piece draws to a close, with no one else there, the sound gradually diminishing and dying out, suspended for a long moment in the atmosphere, you release that last touch on the keyboard and there is nothing left to do because all you ever needed to know, feel and sense has been experienced. Then you're gently reawakened by applause and realise that 700 people were there with you all along, and you've all been on a similar journey.

GERMANY, SEPTEMBER 2016

A German TV show wants to do a feature on me, shot in London and in Cologne. *Instrumental* has just been published over there and I've an upcoming tour so I have to do it. I want to do it. I've always had a strange relationship with Germany. Ever since I was a kid I've been obsessed with the Holocaust. I have a tribute to Auschwitz tattooed on my left wrist, and my son's middle name is Primo, after Levi.

I'm not a practising Jew. I'm not even a full-blooded Jew. I'm Jew-ish. Synagogue makes me puke, having seen the way some of my old friends and family act having sat in synagogue pretending to be all religious and professing to align their actions and beliefs with an apparently benevolent God. No thanks. I haven't set foot in one for decades, even though the music is magnificent – the choir was always the only bit I enjoyed as a kid – soaring, beautiful melodies coming down from God's mouth to my ears, making the immense disparity between the beauty of music and the ugliness of my reality that much starker.

But the Holocaust – that one got right into me. As a teenager I read every book I could find on it, and then went to visit Belsen. My memories of it are of massive lumps in the ground with signs saying '32,000 Jewish children buried here', '12,000 Jewish women buried here' and a silence so deafening that even the birds don't sing. And because I was young and stupid and quick to judge I let it stain my view of Germany today. I immersed myself in the horrors of seventy-five years ago and lost sight of the fact that Germans in 2016 (the vast majority at least) are completely different. My bad. Which is why I'm excited for the tour, to meet people there, to really visit Germany and see the place. Yes, I did just write 'excited' – and I feel it too. I always seem to forget how torturous being on tour can be for me. Concert Day is my very own Groundhog Day.

The film crew arrives and shoot in my tiny flat. They film me walking around Little Venice and on the tube, all of which is mortifying. Wandering around with a team of people with giant cameras on their shoulders, microphones looming over my head, lights being shone at me, suffering the stares of strangers and feeling like a wanker. Whatever. Then they interview me in real depth at home about heavy things and fun things and all the things in between. Like *Salvados*, somehow it's easier speaking about this stuff on camera than when it is live and unedited. I can pretend it's not really real that way. And then two days later I travel to Germany with Denis for the day to do something amazing.

We land in Düsseldorf, then drive to an estate in Cologne. More like a ghetto than an estate. It's filled with high-rise tenement blocks, the walls are splattered with graffiti. And – the irony – there is not a single German face there amongst the locals; instead there are dozens of migrants and refugees – Iranians, Arabs, Poles, Russians – all sitting or standing around a giant grand piano which has been positioned for me out in the open air, bang in the middle of a place that redefines hardship. The crew want to film me playing and chatting with these people about music and life and whatnot. We have a drone camera at our disposal and some of the kids lose their shit with the excitement of seeing it hover above them.

This is exactly what I need. Earlier that morning the actress sent me a text. She seemed to make a point of telling me, in a slightly threatening way, that she was going round to her ex's place for a cup of tea. Something about the words she used makes me think she isn't over him yet. I'm getting better at noticing red flags now, and there have been a few. I'm annoyed, and I'm pissed off with myself that something so trivial is taking up so much space and making so much noise.

I feel way out of my depth, which is the only way I know how to be with a woman. There is such security in the comfortable familiarity of a long-term relationship, even a fucked-up one. I often find myself wondering if going back to one of my exes is the easiest thing to do. But I know deep down that even if I could find one who'd take me back, I couldn't do it. It would be like a recovering alcoholic taking a drink again and thinking that this time it would be different. It's time to move on and hope for something happier and healthier, and that means learning not to freak out when someone doesn't get back to me straight away, not to worry when they're going round to their ex's place to pick up some clothes and have a cuppa, to try and trust that it's all good and moving in the right direction, and if I can't feel like that then to simply walk away, no hard feelings. But really all I feel is idiotic and like the ten-year-old kid at the school disco standing alone and awkward in the corner wondering why he's such a freak.

Being here on this estate, doing something that seems so important, is a good thing. I focus on the job at hand. I sit and play for this random mix of people. I play them a few pieces: some Rachmaninov, some Chopin. They edge closer, staring at the keyboard, filming it, listening, really listening. I don't think most of them have ever seen a piano in real life before.

I ask if anyone plays and an old guy says no but he's always wanted to, so I bring him over, sit him down and show him how to play the first bar of the Bach prelude. His face lights up, gnarled hands repeating bars of Bach and making the piano come alive. It's awesome. A little kid comes up and plays me a piece. I play it back to him, imitating him. We sit down together and play it again, but this time with him playing thumping bass notes and me playing his melody on top of it, improvising on it and embellishing it. It's a connection I couldn't have had with language.

Afterwards, I talk more to some truly inspiring people on the estate. People who have braved uprooting and travelling with nothing but a few sparse possessions to try and find a better, safer life somewhere far away where they don't know the language and, like Orfeo, don't know if they'll even survive, let alone endure or thrive. I realise, once again, just how fucking lucky I am to have such luxury problems.

A young kid brings me flowers. Because he'd seen a movie where someone played the piano on stage and was given flowers afterwards and so he insisted on doing the same thing for me. Which makes my heart melt a little bit. They give me my name in graffiti on a little canvas. Feed me home-made cake. Want pictures and autographs. Introduce me to their dogs and friends and siblings. Until it's almost time to head home. Denis and I go find somewhere that makes schnitzel and has the rudest waiters in the world (that's their 'thing' apparently – it's not personal) before heading back to the airport. I get home in one piece (leaving Denis at Heathrow again – that guy needs a bladder test) and crash for the night.

Two days later we're flying back to Germany so that they can film the live bit of the TV programme with me. It's one of those chat shows where I sit in the middle and am totally surrounded by the audience – my own personal hell. I sit and watch this ten-minute film they've made about me and feel mortified because it talks about my childhood and the rapes and the other weird shit and I'm just sitting there on display like I'm a monkey in some kind of victim zoo. I'm ashamed as I watch it and want the ground to swallow me whole.

After they show the film the host asks me questions in the studio. I'm uncomfortable because it's live, but I remind myself again that although there are hundreds of excuses not to talk about this stuff, there is no single valid reason not to do so. We have to. I have to. It's difficult, but actually we have fun as well when the guy shows me some predictably grim classical album covers and I start laughing at how ridiculous they are and comment that the one with Yo-Yo Ma looks like he's taking a shit and the translator can't speak because he's laughing so hard and the audience aren't quite sure what to make of it and I don't really care because I feel alone and tired and emotional and too fucked to worry. And it's important to find moments to laugh.

Speaking of which, that evening Denis and I go back for more schnitzel, mainly to check on those waiters and see if they were just having a bad day last time. They're even more obstreperous than before. For the second time that day I can't stop laughing, which just makes them even crosser and even ruder. Denis takes a photo of me smoking and giggling. I put it online. The actress sees the photo, sends me a text to say that the photo looks like someone snapped me during a brief moment when I was free of all my shit. And that I looked hot. It feels good. To be reminded that sometimes there can be a chink in the mask and the pain and the so goddam predictable heaviness of life. That there's even proof of it on camera for me to see, if I could just allow myself to believe in it. It also feels good because I am grateful for any scraps of positive attention, even if it comes from some cute too-young girl complimenting me on an Instagram photo. I do a little jig inside. It's amazing how quickly I hand over all the power.

I know this is only a fling. She knows that too – I haven't misled her. It's never going to be anything more and I can actually just relax, lighten up a little bit and enjoy it for what it is – sex, company, lovely trips to fun places, a glorious distraction, a few short weeks of relief and escape.

We go home and this time I actually wait for Denis to take a piss at Terminal 2 before we head through to immigration together, my arm around his shoulder.

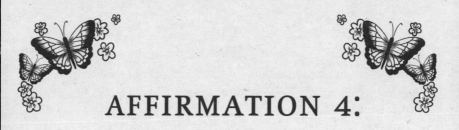

AFFIRMATION 4:

'When you replace
the "I" with "We",
Illness becomes Wellness!'

TRANSLATION:

'I AM BROKEN, EXHAUSTED AND MY LIFE IS FUCKED. DON'T
EVER ASK ANYONE FOR HELP – I'M SAFER ON MY OWN.'

CONCERT PIECE NUMBER FOUR

Beethoven Sonata Op. 110

He had survived, for the large part resentfully, for just over half a century. It is late December in 1821 and Austrian-cold as he stumbles home, cursing the cobblestones and the beer and the ice. A passer-by would perhaps have thought him unwell as he half limps, half walks through the dark Vienna streets mumbling, chatting and occasionally singing to himself. They wouldn't have been wrong – he has been sick for several months. But what they can't know is that this illness is of absolutely no concern to him.

What matters most to him, what causes him a pain few of us could ever imagine, is his total and complete isolation from the world in which he exists. Has always existed. He has felt alone since he was a boy. Beaten and abused, a survivor of an alcoholic and violent father, with too much responsibility foisted on him when he was too young, incapable of anything approaching a functional relationship, enduring financial hardship and depression, weighed down with too much anger. He is gifted unimaginable musical talents by a power greater than anything the human mind can conceive, and then, with a dreadful, cruel irony, he becomes deaf.

He reaches his front door, wasting several frustrating seconds fumbling with his keys. His total lack of social skills mean this is his thirtieth home in just a few years, neighbours and landlords finding him insufferable, immune to his genius. As the door opens, he throws himself over the threshold and lumbers up the stairs. What he lacks in stature he makes up for in personality and, though the house in which he lives is empty, his very presence lights up every room. He produces a kind of ethereal static as he makes his way with a purpose most of us will never comprehend, to his writing desk.

Down he sits. Grabbing his quill and staring at the pieces of paper in front of him, already half obliterated with black ink and almost indecipherable, he starts to write. Not words, though if they had been they would have screamed 'HEAR ME'. But something beneath words. Beyond them. They are quavers, crotchets, semibreves and minims, dynamic markings, interpretive instructions, crescendos, diminuendos, rests, pauses, pedalling suggestions and tempo indications. In the opening six bars of the final movement alone there are twenty-three different directions on how those few bars are to be played. He may be deaf but he knows exactly how he wants it to sound. He writes as though his life depends on it, knowing he has little time left. He writes urgently as if each note is his last. He is permanently tortured by the fact that he has a surplus of ideas and a scarcity of time.

Despite his immensely prolific output, his rapid physical deterioration has meant that the piece he is now composing at his writing desk is the only work he will complete in that entire year. That he is deaf, sick and heartbroken is immaterial compared to what propels him to stay alive. He has a higher purpose and he needs to make it count. It was and is the single, God-driven duty he devoted himself to many years ago, and, digging deep, he hurls onto the page one of the most poignant expressions of grief conceivable to man. He gasps for breath as he scratches the notes down onto the manuscript. Those gasps go into the music, translated into semiquavers and musical slurs, echoing throughout time. When he's too caught up to move and remains frozen, trapped, immutable, then that too goes into the music, with heavily weighted pauses and crushing silences between chords. He bends time to fit his will, expanding or contracting it as and when required. As he cries out to God, asking questions that can only be answered by a force that is wiser and older than humankind, he finds those answers by asking not with words, but in music, his mother tongue.

There are rules to adhere to in composition. Strict and embedded principles and traditions. It has always been this way. But he's beyond the point of sticking to what's expected. His calling transcends what is normal. He rips up the rule book with the sonata he's composing, and the result is the ultimate statement of heroism and survival. It is his very own resurrection, the triumph of hope over suffering.

If only he could mirror that in life. But then again, how could he care about something as mundane and uninspired as life when he is capable of creating music like this?

He finally finishes his 31st Piano Sonata. It is Christmas Day. It is his penultimate sonata. One of the thirty-two that will for ever be studied, listened to and performed in awestruck admiration.

He sets aside the manuscript and pens a note to his friend and benefactor Prince Lichnowsky:

'Prince, what you are, you are by accident of birth,' he writes. 'What I am, I am through my own efforts. There have been thousands of princes and will be thousands more; there is only one Beethoven!'

He writes entirely without arrogance. It is simply his truth.

*

LONDON, SEPTEMBER 2016

I have a meeting today with the head of BBC Radio 3. I've done four shows for them so far and they've been the most enjoyable things I've done in ages. I get to pick ninety minutes of whatever music I want for each show. I then get to introduce those pieces and the performers. As someone on Twitter said after the first broadcast, it's like letting Tigger loose with a gramophone player – my idea of heaven. There is no one in my life with whom I can really share this passion and talk about these pieces, so having a few hundred thousand captive Radio 3 listeners to whom I can vomit out facts and details about the greatest part of my life feels glorious.

At the BBC headquarters Denis makes the fair point to the boss and his director of music that classical music is a bit like golf. He loves golf but just hates almost everyone who plays it. And the clothes. And the sheer fucking whiteness of it all. Classical is the same – the music is so extraordinary but everything surrounding it, from the performers to the promoters, to the dress codes, the rules and air of 'we're so much more refined than you', is pretty vile and has to change. Apparently me talking passionately about my favourite music and musicians on air, with teenage enthusiasm, is actually not a bad thing. The ratings, thankfully, headed north over the course of the four programmes I've done for them and they've had more of a positive reaction on social media than for any other show. They now want me to do a six-pack more. And maybe a few one-off specials. It's an immediate yes from me.

They would also like me to make a documentary about Glenn Gould (TTH™). Denis and I politely agree, but in my head I am losing my shit because, well, Glenn Fucking Gould! I'm going to fly to Toronto and interview people (including, unbelievably, Justin Trudeau), see his piano (Gould's not Trudeau's), *play* his piano, immerse myself in his world. Imagine an F1-obsessed kid hanging out at Lewis Hamilton's house and then driving his McLaren Mercedes around Monaco. Holy shit. Add to that the possibility of exploring Gould in depth and really getting down and dirty with his life. He had too many quirks to list (my favourite being he would often call friends or even vague acquaintances at two in the morning and just talk *at* them all night long even if they slept while he did so – anything to avoid being alone, right?) and is my all-time musical idol. I have a giant photograph of him on my living-room wall. And all of his CDs. And every book ever written about him. And I almost spent £5,000 on his autograph once. But didn't. Still regret not doing so. There is so much I want to explore and find out and speak about regarding the enigma that is Gould.

Most relevant to me right now is how immersed he was with technology. Having retired from performing live while he was still ridiculously young, he became completely obsessed with the whole process of recording and editing. He felt recording was the future and was incredibly skilled at editing, producing and getting to know all the advancing technologies in that field. He was a visionary in that regard – foreseeing Spotify, MP3 players and everything else we so readily take for granted today. He would frequently talk with genuine love about the womb-like security of the recording studio and his 'love affair with the microphone'.

I think of how I'm going to be recording my new album in a few weeks, and see myself there in Snape Maltings, home of Britten, with a beautiful piano, cigarettes, Kit Kats, cups of tea, producer, excellent sound guy, locked doors, soundproofing, Beethoven, Chopin, Rachmaninov, a little cottage next to the studio, reading in the evening, playing piano all day long. I literally can't imagine anything more rewarding, delightful, perfect. And I am not for a second surprised that Gould retired from playing live to focus on recording. Who wouldn't want to ditch the planes and trains and jet lag and risk and memory concerns and anxiety and stage fright for the security of a locked room with a piano in it? Gould was adamant that music must provide shelter from the world, a way to help us all avoid being submerged in it. He got that dead right.

As we leave the BBC offices I'm on a complete high, and I get an email that I'd been hoping for for a while but was not optimistic enough to expect.

The council had been getting more and more aggressive about the 'parking ticket'. It had escalated to the point that they were threatening to destroy the car unless I paid the fine.

Just blow that motherfucker up like a ticking suitcase found at Heathrow. My problem is that the fine is so out of proportion to the crime, the methods they've chosen to chase payment so angry and threatening, that I feel stuck between what I know is right and fair and what I know their lawyers will try and do to me if I don't pay.

After the legal battle surrounding *Instrumental*, I know that mentally I won't survive another court case. Sadly, so do they, hence the level of aggression – they know I'll do anything to avoid ending up in court again. But after much advice and soul-searching I wrote to them suggesting a slightly less extortionate figure to settle the fine once and for all. There was some back and forth but eventually we agreed on a number that hurts but doesn't eviscerate, and that morning, as I leave the BBC, they write to me to accept my offer.

There will not be court proceedings, there will not be lengthy, expensive litigation, I can pay my fine and get on with my life knowing that I need to be much, much more careful about how I drive from now on. I have to remind myself that this is my responsibility. I got the 'ticket', I need to pay it, I need to accept that it's on me, and this is the price I pay for parking like an idiot. Lesson learned. And if I haven't learned it then I'm fucked.

My hope is that now everything is agreed I can move on and let it go. The hard part is over and it's now simply a case of paperwork.

I go home and lose myself in the piano for a couple of hours. Everything else can wait.

It's the perfect moment to tackle head-on a really tricky passage at the end of the *Polonaise-fantasie* that I simply can't get right. I mean, it works about 60 per cent of the time on stage but the other 40 per cent is a bit of a mess. A disaster to me, probably barely noticeable to the audience. But I want it nailed. It's a run of about forty-five notes in the right hand, going as fast as they can from the middle of the keyboard all the way to the top and landing on a giant chord. And while the right hand is doing that super-fast scale, the left hand is playing three chords pretty quickly. Fitting forty-five notes against three chords is a challenge. It's starting to become a bit of a mental block – I know it's coming when I'm on stage and that voice, ever helpful, ever supportive, says 'Here it comes, buddy, you're going to fuck this one up again, uh-oh.' So I hammer away at it for ages. It's amusing and maddening how things seem to be so solid in practice and then so wobbly in performance. But I have all my tricks on how to practise properly (playing it while sitting on the floor instead of the stool, playing it blind-folded, playing it backwards, playing it with different accents and rhythms, playing it silently by touching the keys but not pushing them down, singing it out loud and various other weird and wonderful tips) and apply myself diligently until it feels as failsafe as it can be. Then I go for a walk.

It's a new thing, walking. Obviously I've been doing it since I was ten months old, but the idea of choosing to walk rather than drive, cab or tube is new. I know that it helps me. I've had a good couple of weeks recently, of just about managing my emotions and mood swings, and I am determined to keep the voices at bay. I also blame the iPhone with its step-counting obsession that I've now caught. Unless I do 10,000 steps a day, everything feels wrong (OCD, *moi*?). Today I've only done 6,000.

So I put on my walking shoes, which I've bought especially, and set off. No particular place in general, just walking. Headphones on. Moving away, rather quickly, from my noisy head. Like I've left an angry partner at home and am walking away from her to give us space rather than staying in and talking *at* her for hours, trying to fix the unfixable (much easier to do when you don't actually have a partner and it's all hypothetical).

That's what's so cool about this walking thing. I can plug into music, my body is doing something resembling exercise and I seem to think less. It's a triple win. I only ever listen to one of two albums while I walk. They're both relatively recent ones, having been released in the last year or two. But they have both changed my life for ever. And ever. In fact, I gotta say, they are the single greatest albums of any genre of music that I have ever heard. And I really don't say that lightly. I know I get enthusiastic. I tell people that this pianist is my favourite, or this concert was the best I've *ever* been to, or this book is the greatest since *The Master and Margarita*. You get the idea. But really, truly, these two albums are unlike anything I've heard before in my entire life. And I've heard a lot.

The problem is, they're opera. I know. The art form that's been dying for decades, that has the absolute worst reputation in the classical music world when it comes to snobbishness, inaccessibility and general wankiness. And this in a world where snobbishness is worn like a badge of honour. It's a tough gig to get into.

These two are by Mozart. Which helps. The biggest deterrent to opera, for me, is Wagner. Chubby men and women shrieking at you in German for six hours simply cannot be described as entertainment. Unless you like being bound, gagged and whipped in basement flats in Mayfair. Hence the considerable overlap between these two things in a typical Wagner audience at Covent Garden. I'm sure this is my fault – clearly there's more to it than that – I no doubt simply lack the mental acuity to really *get* Wagner. It's either that or I don't like being flogged. Perhaps one day I will learn to 'appreciate Wagner', as they say. There's no doubt he was one of the great musical geniuses, and I hate missing out on something special, so I'm hopeful.

But Mozart is a different kettle of musical fish altogether. This guy, dead at thirty-five (having composed *two hundred* CD's worth of music), created music that comes straight from God. I *dare* you to argue with me on this. His three greatest operas are *The Marriage of Figaro*, *Così fan tutte* and *Don Giovanni*. Again, try and contradict me on this and see what happens.

It's the first two of these that I'm talking about here – both operas about love with ridiculous storylines, plots, subplots and whatnot. But underneath the farcical stories are important, powerful messages about the nature of love and our capacity for forgiveness. And Mozart sets these stories to the most profound music imaginable.

The key problem with classical music is that it is only ever as good as the performance you are hearing or witnessing. It's the same with theatre. On paper something can be one of the seven wonders of the world, but performed by certain people it becomes a kind of torture. Beyond the hypothetical, a work of art can only ever be as good as its interpreter. Which is why Gould, von Karajan, Horowitz, Callas, Sokolov etc. are all so immortal. They are capable of reimagining what has been set down on paper hundreds of years earlier and offering it to audiences in the present day in a way that is entirely captivating and profound.

So along comes a young Greek conductor called Teodor Currentzis. This guy is the conducting equivalent of Glenn Gould morphed with Kurt Cobain. Gould said, perhaps famously, there is no point playing something that's been performed a thousand times before unless you do it differently. And Currentzis, who has a work ethic and attention to detail that makes Bill Gates look like a bum who spends his days watching daytime TV with a can of Special Brew and an ashtray balanced precariously on his chubby thighs, goes way, way beyond that. He formed his own orchestra, hand-selecting the very best musicians he could find, largely from Russia where they have quite the selection, and called it MusicAeterna (Latin for eternal, and boy are they).

He somehow convinced Sony to inject an obscene amount of money, and he set to work producing and creating new and definitive performances of Mozart's three greatest operas. He records in Perm, Russia, a tiny town, the gateway of Siberia where the temperature redefines cold. He, his orchestra and singers along with producers, sound engineers etc. spend a couple of weeks in what can only be described as a classical music lock-in – they live, eat and breathe (and occasionally sleep) there all together, and the majority of their waking moments are spent creating music. Hundreds of hours of takes are recorded, with Currentzis rarely if ever satisfied, going again and again and pushing everyone involved beyond the limits of what most people would consider possible. Speeds that are, to many, unplayable. Vocal techniques not taught in any schools (singing while eating, singing in comically fake voices and more). Interpretations that would make most music critics and regular opera audiences question everything they thought they knew. His conceptions of these works are so grand, so life-affirming and life-changing, so far beyond anything that has come before it that it has, for me, redefined music itself.

I found the first two albums – *Figaro* and *Così* – by dumb luck and have, quite literally, spent hundreds of hours listening to these two operas in particular. They accompany me everywhere. I've listened to them so frequently that I dream about them. Oftentimes, especially when overtired and drowsy, it is the arias of *Figaro* or *Così* that replace the voices in my head now. Which is a much safer bet. I'm anxiously waiting for *Don Giovanni*, which will be out imminently.

There is no other album I have heard where I know, just absolutely know, that this is how the composer himself would have heard it in his head while he was writing it down on paper. It's as if Currentzis has found some cosmic wormhole, tunnelled back in time into Mozart's mind and replicated what Mozart was thinking in the present day. A freak teleporting of genius from across the space/time continuum. Everything about it is outrageously good – the attack of the strings, the unbelievably immediate presence of the sound where the listener feels like they are sitting right in the middle of the orchestra as melody after melody sweeps through their ears, the quality of the singing, the sheer, visceral, driving energy of the whole thing, the humour, originality, pathos, romance, verve, face-punching force of it all . . . It is completely overwhelming. This is classical music breaking the four-minute mile.

One of my favourite stories about *Così* (I've started something now and am getting all giddy – bear with me) is that the librettist, Lorenzo Da Ponte, had a mistress for whom he wrote one of the main roles. Mozart loathed her. And he noticed that when she sang high notes she would lift her face to the sky and when she sang low notes she would drop her chin down to her chest. So while he was writing her famous, showcase aria, '*Come scoglio*' ('Like a Rock' – she's saying that she's going to be completely faithful to her fiancé, the lying bitch) he fills the whole thing with jumps from high to low and low to high, in order, in Mozart's own words, 'to make her head bob up and down on stage like a chicken'.

I think of Mozart conducting this, watching the soprano nodding her head up and down and giggling to himself. Most amazing to me is the fact that Mozart composes one of the greatest and most beautiful operatic arias ever, while simultaneously taking the piss out of a girl he detested. This is the closest classical music gets to thug life.

The plot of *Così* is worth telling. In brief (you're welcome), two guys are engaged to two girls. Everyone loves each other very much. Then a pal of the two men by the name of Don Alfonso (very Mafia) suggests that actually *all* women are liars and cheaters, and true, faithful love doesn't exist. The guys are understandably affronted and so a bet is made: Don Alfonso says give him twenty-four hours and he'll prove that the girls are just like all other women (*Così fan tutte* is translated as 'Women are like that', a rather gratingly misogynist throwback), provided the two guys do exactly as he asks. They agree, certain that they're going to make some easy money.

A plan is hatched that entails the two men (who are soldiers) telling their beloveds that they've been urgently called off to war. There's much wailing and gnashing of teeth but off they go, the girls promising to love them for ever, etc. etc. Shortly thereafter (hours not days) they return – and here's the retarded bit – wearing fake moustaches and pretending to be Albanian pirates. They then try and woo the girls (swapping partners in the process), and the girls (who don't recognise them at all because, well, they're really good fake moustaches), end up doing exactly what Don Alfonso said they would. It takes them a few hours, but sure enough they succumb, the two men are understandably distraught and, to make matters worse, the women now, unbelievably, agree to marry the 'Albanians' (bear in mind this is all happening within a twenty-four-hour period) and a wedding is quickly arranged. A fake notary is used, the girls think they're actually married and then, boom, all is revealed. And rather than saying 'fuck you' and running away as fast as possible, the two men forgive the women (because, don't forget, 'All women are like that'), everyone falls back in love with the right people and the entire group (literally) sings the praises of accepting a life that is filled with good and bad and ups and downs.

I mean, really.

But dig a little deeper and it's about so much more than fidelity and facial hair. At the time Mozart wrote it, love was held up as some kind of super-romantic, sacred ideal. The idea of fallibility and the human condition was disallowed when it came to love. I like to think Mozart wanted to use this opera to make it a bit clearer that we are all indeed human, that love is not some flawless paradigm and the notion of perfect love is completely unsustainable. That all of us have inconsistent feelings when it comes to love and everyone is capable of cheating, lying, inflicting hurt.

Figaro's story is equally idiotic. There is infidelity, mistaken identity, cross-dressing, the whole shebang. But again, there is a much deeper reality here. The ending makes me sob (in Currentzis's hands) every time. In fact, many times I just can't listen to the last few tracks because I genuinely think I'll throw myself under a train. If you ever need a really good cry, then this is your guaranteed snot-fest.

(I was, amusingly, about to hesitate to write the following because it contains plot spoilers. But then I thought if anyone reading this is genuinely upset by an opera spoiler then please get in touch and let's be best friends. Because clearly, and perhaps sadly, no one else will really give two fucks, and the fact that you do is amazing to me in a really good way.)

Figaro's boss, the Count, doesn't deserve the 'o' in his title. He is trying to cheat on his lovely wife, the Countess, with his manservant Figaro's fiancée Susanna (on their wedding day, natch). He thinks he's getting away with it too. Until right at the end when, after much trickery, dishonesty and bullshit, he's exposed, and the woman he's trying to shag turns out not to be Susanna at all but is, in fact, his actual wife (they meet in the garden, the Count thinking he's on a promise, but Susanna is actually the Countess in disguise – a really good one, despite the lack of moustaches). But here's the kicker: he suddenly realises he's fucked up. And fucked up good and proper. His wife has known all along that he was trying to shag another woman and he's been caught red-handed.

There is a moment of total silence. The whole mood changes in a heartbeat. The audience and cast are freeze-framed and tense.

He drops to his knees, all pretence and cockiness instantly evaporated, and sings one of the most beautiful, pleading, desperate arias I've ever heard, 'Contessa perdono!' – 'Countess, forgive me!'. And the Countess, more kind than he ('Più docile io sono' – 'I am more mild'), without hesitation forgives her husband. Just like that. This is the moment where I can't stop the tears. She's been humiliated, hurt, treated like shit for years and then, suddenly, when he begs her forgiveness she immediately grants it. Because, simply, she loves him. There are no recriminations, point-scoring, anger, judgement. Just love and an open heart. As the music gently and oh so beautifully reveals her mercy, appearing behind her comes the whole cast and chorus and they all join in, singing the most transcendent, celebratory music, floating down from heaven and echoing the Countess's forgiveness, signalling the universal spiritual message of compassion, love and redemption. The lyrics they sing can be roughly translated as:

> 'Ah! All shall be
> made happy thereby.
> Only love can resolve
> this day of torments,
> caprice and folly,
> into joy and happiness.'

Love does indeed conquer all.

This opera always *really* gets to me. I look back at some of my relationships, one in particular, where I've acted like a dick and hurt people and refused to see my part in things because I will do anything rather than take responsibility for my actions, and it's so much easier to blame the other person all the time and I see that I was the C(o)unt then. Not by cheating, but in myriad other manipulative, dishonest and deceptive ways.

A few years ago I had had an agonising break-up with my then girlfriend. I was in another country with my very young son, staying in a shitty, snowed-in hotel. He kept asking why his mother and I had divorced with such desperation in his voice, and why I couldn't live there with them, why I couldn't buy a house in the same street and he could come and visit me every day, why his mum had taken him to live all the way across the world. I just wanted to die. I called my recently ex-girlfriend to whom I had been such an asshole. She talked me down gently, guided me through what I had to do over the coming few days (I was genuinely in real emotional trouble and only just about capable of following simple instructions) and was waiting for me at 6 a.m. at Heathrow when I returned four days later. No blame, no 'I told you so', no 'You owe me big time, asshole', just love, compassion, forgiveness and the Countess in the garden saying of course I forgive you because what matters is love, real love, big fat juicy love.

Even writing this, let alone listening to this put to music and played like a GOD by Currentzis and his orchestra, I'm crying. Because I don't feel like I deserve that kind of love, that degree of kindness, and when it comes (rare, but it does come like it did that early morning at Heathrow), I don't know what to do with it other than absolutely block out any level of trust in it and assume it's all a trick. That's why I'm divorced, twice. And my exes and friends call me the 'anti-trust guy'. I hate it but I don't know any better and I'm trying so goddam hard to rewire that part of my brain that was so appallingly betrayed when I was a little boy while it was still plastic and being formed and now will not, cannot, must not ever, ever, ever trust people.

Currentzis, however, I trust wholeheartedly. And I've never even met him. His albums have become my best friends. They offer me everything I've ever wanted – a deeper understanding of myself, a beauty that is unimaginable, a window onto another world that is better, safer, more profound and filled with more meaning than the one I currently inhabit. He keeps me company while I walk. And ride the tube. And make dinner. And during the lonely post-divorce nights. And in the car, on planes, in hotels, backstage, on (too rare) holidays. He is the perfect partner, one who is incapable of betrayal. Buy his albums, I beg you.

Enough about opera.

For now.

Back to me walking. I find myself in Marylebone and close to the Steinway showroom. George, one of the sales guys, is there. I love George. He gets in early every day to practise his singing before they open up, he's kind and funny, and happy to let me play their pianos. I ask him if they have a free room for me to practise in and, surprisingly, they do. I usually have to call and book ahead. I go down into the basement where they have their workshop and a couple of practice rooms. It's like a piano graveyard down there, the back room in *Six Feet Under* – carcasses of mahogany, tools, saws, the smell of varnish, the insides of pianos, their guts spilled out to be renovated, restrung, brought back to life. It's full of technicians who look like they've never seen daylight, furiously working away. I like to think nothing has changed here for a hundred and fifty years. A bit like the Wigmore Hall audience.

This is the place where out-of-town pianists can come and practise. And, more importantly, find another basement they feel safe in, perhaps make a couple of new friends and hang out with like-minded freaks like me. It's my safe place. A musical haven in the heart of London where I can find people to talk to about split octaves and double thirds, eavesdrop on other pianists and, occasionally, meet some of my heroes who are in town preparing for a Prom or Barbican recital.

I walk into Studio One, catching the sounds of Chopin coming from Studio Two, and sit at the piano. I get my hands warm and then I play through the whole concert programme from start to finish. The Bach Prelude in C major, the Chopin *Fantasie* in F minor, the Chopin *Polonaise-fantasie*, the Beethoven Sonata Op. 110, the Rachmaninov Prelude Op. 32/13 and the Gluck Melody from *Orfeo*. And it all fits right. Memory is fine, the notes are solid, the sound deep. It takes me just over an hour, and by the end I'm feeling more confident, more relaxed and have a slight sense of having accomplished something.

I walk back home, *Figaro* keeping me company, I'm excited about my playing, about the new Radio 3 shows I am going to do and, most of all, relieved that I've finally managed to resolve the 'parking ticket' without ending up in court. All my plates are in the air but they're still spinning and feel well balanced. And I'm not even sitting at a piano.

This is the best I've felt in ages. I may have turned some kind of a corner. At last.

BILBAO, OCTOBER 2016

They like me in Spain. Well, that's how it feels to me. I still can't get over it. Someone sending me a nice email makes my day. A pretty girl smiling at me on the tube makes my week. An entire country making me feel welcomed and loved and good – well, that's something else entirely.

I'm here in Bilbao to be interviewed and play the piano on stage tomorrow as part of a festival. It's called Ja! Bilbao, and is dedicated to humour in literature. Obviously *Instrumental*, a book about classical music, child rape, suicide and mental illness, fits right in there. The truth is, there are, I hope, some funny moments in the book, intentional or otherwise. I didn't survive and get vaguely well to be a miserable fuck (all the time) and I'm thrilled the humour in the book has come through.

The hotel is literally opposite the Guggenheim Museum. Denis is with me again and, as per usual, after checking into the hotel at 7 p.m., we head off to find something to eat way too early by Spanish standards. We find a deserted restaurant that's open and slightly astonished we want to have dinner and not lunch, and this time we try and order things from the Spanish menu. We've been coming to this country a lot now and we're feeling a little braver.

However, it's fair to say we have mixed success with this. I blame Denis. He pretends he's all au fait with the language and, like a dad with a satnav, ignores the friendly waitress who offers to translate for him, and orders something called *percebes* a bit too confidently which, when they arrive, look like tiny alien foetuses. As he nonchalantly tries to eat one, pretending to know exactly what he's doing, it explodes, and it looks like a barnacle has just pissed all over him. I end up with something that looks like cod but I'm not sure. It's an unusual colour. Neither of us acknowledges the fact that we have absolutely no idea what we're eating, and down it goes anyway because it's fuel and my body needs it.

Throughout the meal we don't stop talking. Denis asks me important questions like do I ever fart on stage (only in the loud bits). Mainly we talk about girls (how, what, why – but mainly how) and business. After thirty-seven minutes I pay the bill and we boost, stopping at an ice cream place where I get one scoop and Denis gets three (taking ten minutes to decide which flavours and pretending he hasn't had an ice cream in a year, which is a glaring fucking lie as we had one in Madrid last month). We sit and I smoke and we talk some more. I share with him the little worries and anxieties I can't talk to anyone else about without them looking at me like I smell funny.

I tell him about the actress, about how I need to protect her and me from the inevitability of what's to come: possessiveness (me), cruelty (me), confusion (her), hurt (her). I can't go through all this again. How can I aspire to act respectfully and compassionately around someone when it takes such a huge effort to do the same for myself? Denis, who has witnessed several of my relationship breakdowns, smiles and just nods in his lovely, wise, non-judgemental way.

There's a slight sense of panic inside me despite the relaxed nature of the evening. I guess it's to do with the actress, with being on tour and Concert Day looming. Although it's not even a proper concert. I'll be discussing my book on stage, there will be simultaneous translation (the audience wearing headphones) and, as they always do, they've brought in a piano and want me to play. At least it's on a real piano. Sometimes festivals bring an electric keyboard because budget or space forbids a real piano. And for the odd, simple piece that's fine. But it's a weird thing for me. I can't imagine a chef being interviewed about his book and then given a microwave and told to make a fucking bouillabaisse, but if I say no to an electric keyboard and insist on a proper piano I feel like a diva. Another reason it's great having Denis, who can easily play bad cop, by my side.

Regardless, I'm worried about how it will pan out and that I won't sleep well. Won't sleep at all. I tell Denis I need to get back to the hotel for an early night. He understands because he's probably the closest person to me in the world and he's vaguely stable and manages to somehow hold all my difficult feelings without making me feel like a freak. I'm not quite sure how he does it but he does, consistently. It must be like hanging out with a frightened puppy who's been badly beaten when he was younger – occasionally ready to be loved and stroked and then, without warning, completely withdrawn and shut down and snarling at you in the corner.

I close the hotel room door and fall into bed with my Kindle to read something easy and fast, then I pass out, albeit temporarily.

Sure enough, I wake up too many times in the night to count. I haven't had one of my nightmares but I still feel like I've not had any sleep at all. So I let Denis hit the Guggenheim at 10 a.m. while I wake up slowly. At 11 we meet downstairs because there's a singer-songwriter who's flown up from Barcelona to meet with us. I want to sign her to my record label (formed as a labour of love as I'm fed up with the usual music industry bullshit). She's brilliant and unique and has something new to say. She reminds me of Kate Bush fused with Joanna Newsom – all weirdly ethereal vocals laid over simple, beautiful instrumentation. It'll be my first signing, although the label has been going for over a year and a half. The legal case around *Instrumental* took it out of me somewhat and it's taken this long for me to start to focus on things other than the essentials (concerts, practising, staying alive).

In fact, I'm so focused on her that when she asks me what I'm going to play at the festival, I realise that I genuinely haven't got a clue. Imagine that. Me, the ultimate control freak, just letting it all unfold naturally, knowing I've got at least seventy-five minutes of music in my head and fingers and only need to find thirty or so later on. I don't know what happened to stop my usual patterns of obsessive thinking but I could definitely get used to that feeling of freedom. Not having my head full to bursting with intrusive thoughts, double-checking memory, having to engage in 'conversations' with the voices while I'm halfway through playing the difficult bits of a Beethoven sonata in my head, pretending to be present with those around me while urgently trying to remember the facts, figures and anecdotes I'm going to be talking about that night and making sure they all make sense, that they all fit right so that the jigsaw puzzle of music and chat resembles something vaguely meaningful and in line with the theme I've chosen, then anxiously wondering about the piano, the audience, wrong notes, memory lapses, hairs on the keys, disguising my grunting, squeaking and sniffing on stage, is this the evening where I'm finally unmasked as a massive fucking fraud, the signing, the dinner afterwards, being too tired, not sleeping that night, what time I have to be at the airport the next day, will there be press, have I called my mum, is Denis happy enough, will I be happy enough.

I haven't thought about all that because I've been distracted – the festive atmosphere, Bilbao, the singer, the food, the promoters' enthusiasm . . . Enjoying the moment. Last night's panic has disappeared. I feel that people here believe in me even if I don't believe in myself, and by an odd kind of osmosis that sense of belief is maybe seeping into me, for once.

The interview starts off really well. I play the little Bach prelude to begin with, and then the interviewer and I start chatting. It's a strange thing mixing up an interview with playing. It's probably why virtually no other idiot does the whole talking thing at their concerts – it borders on schizophrenia moving from playing to talking to playing and back again. I think it takes such an immense amount of focus just to remember all the musical notes and move into that performance zone, that interrupting it between pieces and talking makes it ten times harder. But hey, I've only got myself to blame.

It's all going swimmingly until the interviewer starts to read passages from my book. They're quite dark passages – one about a suicide attempt, one about my visceral sense of self-hatred and wanting to die. In context they make sense in the book. But somehow hearing them being read out on stage, even in Spanish, with no framework, no explanation, feels dreadful. I feel completely exposed and ashamed, just like during the live German TV interview.

But I get over it, reminding myself why I wrote about all that in the first place, change the subject slightly to make it less victim-oriented and, of course, play more pieces on the piano. I come off the stage feeling better. It's inevitable, I think – my past follows me wherever I go; I've made the choice, with the best possible motives, to put it out there, and it's going to be around for a while. And it is important to own it and not shy away from it. Even if that means much of my family have barely spoken to me since *Instrumental* came out and almost none of them have read it or ever even mentioned it. It's sad and surprising how people react to hearing the truth. Secrecy is a difficult habit to break.

I'm determined not to let the rumbling voices get the upper hand. And then, as if by magic, and just when I most need it, John Cleese appears. He is headlining the festival. He's one of the people who radically improved my life when I was younger, who made me laugh like a drain when I was in dire need of doing so. I go say hello and thank you and he's so goddam charming. We chat for a while and I give him a couple of CDs because he asks me for them. I really want to say to him 'I hope you love these so much you tweet about them and tell all your buddies to buy them and hire me to play at fancy parties' but end up just saying 'I really hope you enjoy these.' I am getting better at hiding my overwhelming neediness at times.

I am, slowly, coming to realise that there is a middle ground in relationships somewhere between shutting down completely and being hyper-needy. The fact that I'm learning this at this stage in my life would make me laugh if it weren't so pathetically sad. I'm almost certain most people figure this stuff out in their teens. I want, more than I want anything else in my life, to find someone I can trust. To have a relationship where I know and accept that I have no right to control the other person's life, where I can gently let go of someone even while I'm with them and trust that they may still stick around and be there and not end up despising me. That's what I'm looking for. One day. That's when things will soften and open, and start to feel safe. If that's possible and it does indeed happen I think it'll be the making of me.

I'm not there yet though. I realise that the fling with the actress I'm seeing has to end. I'm not ready for anything like this. I thought I could do a short few weeks of sex, adventures and fun times. I did all of that with her but then the feelings came too, and with them the need to have her all to myself *for ever*, together with her constant reassurance that she was crazy about me. And of course she wasn't. Because I'm much older than her, mental, my hair is shit, I've no sense of fashion, can't dance and don't drink. And we'd only been on a handful of dates.

So that night, back in London and before flying to Hanover for the first half of my German tour, I call her to end things. It has been two months, and I realise that, even taking into account my own crazy, no matter how hot she is, me and 27-year-olds don't mix. I've rarely felt so old or uncool, and deep down I know that pulling the plug is the safest option. I haven't dealt with the fallout from my divorce, and I don't know if I'm coming or going on a daily basis. I've been a fucking idiot. She takes it remarkably well. Gets a little angry. Then goes out all night drinking. Can't say I blame her.

After we talk I lie in bed in my flat, running through the Germany shows in my head. I am trying to ignore the faint, insistent voice that is telling me I'll be single forever.

I get up and pace, and listen to Teodor Currentzis at 2 a.m. because that's all I've got. And actually, it's not such a bad deal being in a relationship with music rather than with a girl. I get to listen to music like this, I get to play the compositions I've loved and worshipped all my life on amazing pianos in beautiful halls, I get to travel around Germany, Spain, Colombia, Argentina, Australia, America, Mexico. The composers whose works I study and worship are always there for me. It's the best kind of relationship. I'm not going to fuck Brahms's head up by constantly asking him if I'm his favourite interpreter and does he like any other pianists, and is he sure, and am I really good enough and why did he mention that other pianist FIVE YEARS AGO if he didn't like him more than me and what exactly did he say to all the other pianists he's listened to and how can I believe him when he tells me I'm his favourite and fuck him and I'm out of here and you're a cunt.

If the only way to be free of all that relationship bollocks is to be single and alone, then as long as I've got music beside me, it's totally worth it. I fall asleep instantly.

GERMANY TOUR PART 1, OCTOBER 2016

Bilbao was a tonic. Moments of respite from my head, shifting the spotlight onto the singer-songwriter for a bit, avoiding a full-on panic attack and being more relaxed about my event was all so refreshing. Ending a relationship is never fun, but having a few quiet days to myself back home in London has helped too. The only fly in the ointment is not sleeping more than three or four hours a night, but hey, still no nightmares, so I can't be too fussy.

On the morning I fly back to Germany, I wake up trying really, really hard to cling on to Mr Optimistic and to make sure his voice drowns the others'. I adjust my head accordingly, trying to accept the reality of being single and, thanks to the cost of sorting out the 'parking ticket', broke for a while – and to not worry too much that I haven't had enough sleep. I want to make the most of this tour in Germany. I'm playing initially in four cities in four days to people who have paid money, actual money, to come and see me perform. In Germany! Home of my heroes from Bach to Brahms to Schumann.

I arrive at Heathrow staggeringly early, of course. Some things will never change. The flight is at 6.05 p.m. and right now it's 2 p.m. I don't know why I do it. It's like people who correct other peoples grammar. It's a compulsion. A sickness, if you will. In my case it's born of fear. What if the train is delayed, the plane leaves early (I know), there's a three-hour queue at security and on and on.

I keep reminding myself how lucky I am, but try as I might I can't keep it up, this positivity. Airports are lonely places at the best of times, and today it's particularly grim, with thoughts of the actress, exes, my bachelor future invading my mind.

I know the two best things I can do right now are firstly, stay away from security for the time being as I'll want a cigarette as close to boarding as possible. And secondly, listen to music. I fancy a specific performance of the Tchaikovsky Violin Concerto (amazing piece, Currentzis conducting in unimaginably brilliant fashion, as ever) as it seems to fit with my mood. I don't have it on my phone but I press a few buttons and within four seconds it's downloading (what a time to be alive!) and I'm listening as I sit and watch people go by. I start to feel a bit calmer.

After a while, (the twenty-minute first movement), I have my smoke, suffer the indignity of airport security, and find myself in Terminal 5. I remind myself that I need to eat as I've not done that yet today, even though it's now 3 p.m. I go sit in Giraffe and order a full English breakfast. Being in Giraffe reminds me of happier times when I'd take my son there for pancakes and sausages (not the one at Heathrow, obvs), and I allow myself to indulge in a few minutes of daydreaming. I miss him so much.

I can only eat a third of my meal. The waitress gently scolds me. Smiles at me and tells me no wonder I'm so thin if I leave that much food on my plate. Out of nowhere, a voice in my head starts shouting, 'You pathetic scrawny heap of shit, what's wrong with you? Eat like a man,' because I'm in that kind of zone now. I still tip her 30 per cent because I want her to like me and I feel guilty I've turned her into a nasty bitch in my head.

I wander around buying toothpaste and Imodium (as we

all know by now, concert days can be terrifying for me and sometimes have explosive physical repercussions). I clock all the couples doing last-minute shopping before their holiday. I feel nauseous. Airports seem to turn up the volume on feelings and I'm feeling very sorry for myself. Look at me: none of my ex-wives is here. The actress I was dating isn't here. I'm alone and unable to share my life with anyone, not even my own son (albeit for reasons I can't control). I tell myself that this is all I am ready for right now. This is my life and it's actually OK. But the feeling that I've become married to my job, and that I can't even fuck it or take it shopping for duty-free, is doing my head in now.

I sit down on a random bench and email my new shrink. She's a good one – older, wiser, kinder, loving. I jettisoned the dodgy one a few weeks previously. In my first session with her I sat on her couch and sobbed with rage. I told her it is clear, aged forty-one, that I am incapable of having a healthy relationship. Her response, quite simply and without judgement, was that given all that has happened, it's no surprise. In a way, this makes it ten times worse. Because once again we're back to the victim thing.

'Given all that has happened'.

It drives me literally mad. The idea that because this guy raped me for years, because I got slightly broken physically and mentally, it's a miracle that as an adult I can get myself dressed and show up for work, let alone even attempt any kind of relationship. But a healthy relationship? God, no. That's going to take years to learn how to do. It's a particularly vicious circle for me – I get furious at the impact of my past on my present;

I struggle in the present, and try to understand why by looking back on my past; I see that, any way you look at it I genuinely was a victim; I realise the heavy price I'm still paying for my past today; I'm furious at the impact of my past on my present. And round and round it goes. I didn't know whether to punch the wall of my new shrink's office or just properly break down on her floor and not get up.

But I didn't do either because the anger isn't safe to let out and never will be. And I can't break down in front of her. I just can't. Because I don't think I'll ever get back up if I do. I've never, ever, expressed the real extent of the anger I hold inside to anyone, in or out of therapy. Not consciously anyway. Even in the safe confines of a locked ward it didn't feel safe. I explained this to her and she listened and heard me and seemed to understand. There were no trite clichés and promises of a better future. Just a calm assertion that together we will make sure I don't repeat the same old patterns and get into long-term relationships with unsuitable people. She reassured me that forty-one is young, there's much that's worth celebrating in my life and that I'm doing important things in many areas, both workwise and also personally. She seemed to see the good in me and was able to point it out to me in a way that felt genuine and honest. She told me that she can help me look at the 'dark stuff' safely. And that together we can move through it. Surprisingly, I believed her.

In my email to her, I explain about the hole inside me that's threatening to eat me alive here in Terminal 5, that I would rather have anyone/anything to fill it than just sit there with it. I suggest, rather desperately, resuming things with the actress or just finding someone, anyone, new for a few weeks. And an hour later she writes back:

'I think you know the answer to this. You have to fill this black empty hole *before* you begin another relationship or resume the one you've just left. It's always been there but has been covered up with trauma, pain and hurt and most of all grief for what has been lost so long ago – Innocence. It's a real chance to heal yourself and to become attached in a healthy way. Enjoy your concerts and be splendid, as indeed you are. Courage my friend!'

Innocence lost. That's the root of my troubles, I think. Of course the opposite of innocence is guilt. I have been guilty all of my life. I'm not talking about the feeling of guilt. I don't feel guilt, I feel shame. But I am guilty as in I've been convicted of a crime for which I am now paying the price. And that means prison time. A lot of it. Which is why I am here, alone, depressed, having tried to eat rancid eggs in another fucking airport with two failed marriages and a tonne of baggage/red flags for anyone stupid enough to consider dating me.

With exquisite timing, the actress decides this second to send me a goodbye selfie. As if to remind me of what I've just thrown away. She looks immaculate in the way only young, sexually relaxed, confident women can be. Instead of ignoring it I of course immediately decide that I have to return serve and send her one back. I take thirty-four pictures of myself, then proceed to delete each one in disgust. This is nearly a new low for me. Sitting down trying all kinds of different facial expressions (cool, aloof, penetrating, focused, smiling, casual, angry, pouting, sleepy, chilled, sexy, blue fucking steel) and each one makes me want to run up to the nearest armed policeman shouting 'Allahu Akbar' with a wire coming out of my jacket. I'd gone on a date once with a millennial. She took an effortless, amazing selfie (this is apparently normal during a date). I then tried to do the same and she just laughed and said, sweetly, 'Oh baby, you just *have* to find your angle.' I had nothing to say to that. It's a different universe.

I shuffle to the gate and start to board. I've paid for row 7. Paying to choose a seat on a plane when you've already bought a ticket: added to the list of things that make me want to die. It has to be an aisle seat (quick getaway) and as close to the front as possible (ditto). I sit down, plug in (Currentzis's *Figaro* – again), and wait fifty-nine minutes for the plane to take off and land in Hanover.

I get to the hotel and discover that it is the biggest shithole in Europe with a room that I can barely fit my suitcase in and the tiniest single bed I've ever seen.

To make things even more fun, I'm really anxious. I worry about the tour. No one knows who the fuck I am here, except a small bunch of dedicated fans and some random people who have seen me in the press here or watched the TV show I did a few weeks ago. The German edition of *Instrumental* is selling quite well, but some markets are slow burners, no one here knows what to expect from me during a concert as I've never played in this country before and the promoters are not going to be making much money. I'd be surprised if any of the venues are more than half full. Or half empty, depending on what frame of mind you're in. And we all bloody know what frame of mind I'm in. Mr Optimistic definitely left the house hours ago – or he is hiding somewhere in the attic ready to top himself. Mr Worry has taken over.

The tour manager, Elke, offers me dinner out. I say no because I know I won't be good company. I ask at the front desk if they have room service and am met with a stare of incomprehension. So I order a Domino's pizza (seriously) to be delivered to the room (cell) and wait for it lying on my tiny single bed and watching arguably the greatest TV show of all time, *Friday Night Lights*.

It's magnificent television and a show that everyone should watch even if the premise (Texas small town American high school football team) makes you want to puke. Because it's about so much more than American football. I find myself in pieces every eighteen minutes – the music, the inspiration and aspiration, the football coach being there for his boys, the idea of something uniting whole communities and people chasing their passions. Most of all it's the relationship between the coach and his wife (kind, honest, intimate, long-term, human, open, gentle, forgiving) that makes me weep. In a good way, for once. I swear box sets are usually far more effective than antidepressants. Cheaper too. Sleep comes eventually.

Luckily, the next day is a better one. I feel OK when I wake up; the black dog has gone for a walk. When I arrive for a soundcheck at the venue I'm alarmed because the piano is small. Still a grand, but much smaller than the concert grand I'd been expecting. However the acoustics are terrific and the piano sound itself is wonderful. I walk on stage for the concert feeling relaxed, not too nervous, not feeling like I'm performing to a group of hostiles. I wonder if speaking in English will be a disaster, if they'll heckle, walk out, throw things. But they understand me (of course they do, it's only we English who are shit at other languages) and they laugh when they're meant to, right from the start. The audience is dead quiet while I'm playing, not a single mobile phone going off, pure attention, barely any coughing, despite the hall being full (after all that). I play well. I never feel like I play well for a whole concert. But tonight I did. Either my expectations have gone down or there is a growing sense of self-belief, and my moods of desperation are perhaps fewer and further between.

At the end I play a couple of encores to this completely focused crowd. I do my book and CD signing to a surprising number of people and then am back at the hotel, cramming myself into my tiny bedsit of a room while Elke gets me a cheeseburger – my post-concert dish of choice, as ever. It's nearly 11 p.m. by the time I start to eat and, as usual, I sit going through each note of the concert while I munch, slightly ashamed at the carb and saturated fat overdose, seeing and noting where I can improve, what needs to be worked on, which bars were less successful than others and why.

I'm always wired after a concert. It takes me a long time to come down from the adrenalin high. I've been told this is common and especially prevalent in someone like me who has experienced a lot of early trauma (ugh, here we go again with the sad me). The receptors in the brain which control adrenalin and dictate the fight, flight or freeze response operate at such an intense level when there is constant fear in childhood (or the battlefield – same thing in certain cases) that they lose, over time, the ability to regulate things effectively. Which means that my adrenalin levels are almost always at an unusually high intensity. It's why I jump out of my skin at sudden noises, Vietnam-vet style. Once there is a flood of it in my system it doesn't normalise itself well, and rather than draining away over time it just kind of stays there, making my heart beat like a fucked clock, thoughts racing through my head, body shaking. It's no fun being alone at times like this. And yet it's equally awkward being with someone when you look slightly crazed and feel constantly like you're in an ambush in Fallujah.

I drift into sleep around 5 a.m. and am up at 9 a.m. to get ready for the drive to Berlin.

It's been thirty-six hours of sadness, optimism, pleasant surprises and feeling slightly detached from reality. Or as the rest of the world calls it, 'Tuesday'. I sit in the front of the car with Elke and doze as we listen to David Hasselhoff songs on Bob! Radio (fuck me) and head to Potsdam for a live radio interview on the way to Berlin. At the start of the interview they play the whole of Pulp's 'Disco 2000' (it's a rock station evidently), chat with me and then say it's time for some Bach. I get so excited because I'm in Germany, home of my musical heroes, and they're going to play the Aria from the Goldberg Variations performed by Glenn Gould on a rock station, and as the Aria starts I think 'Man, this country is cultured', but after thirteen seconds the presenter cuts it off and goes back to talking. Classical music: a universal herpes.

We drive on to Berlin. Check in at the hotel. It's much nicer, we've upgraded from one to four stars now and the room has a beautiful view of the river and of some astonishing architecture. Over the next hour I drive to the venue, notice it's not a Steinway, freak out, realise it's a fucking massive Bechstein in terrific shape, try it, fall in love with it, get giddy with joy about playing it, and then head back to the hotel for a couple of hours' rest as it's a 9 p.m. start rather than 8 p.m., and hanging out at the venue would make me too itchy.

I'm thinking it's going to be OK, that I can do this, when out of the blue, as I'm pacing around my room, I start getting text messages about the 'parking ticket'. It throws me completely. They'd agreed and signed off on the fine and now they seem intent on wanting to change the terms of the deal we agreed, trying to drag things out a bit longer, making snide comments, rubbing my face in it. I'm so fragile I know I'm in real danger of freaking out but I can't afford to so close to the concert. I have to put the fire out. I try calling my best pal Matthew, Denis and my shrink but they're not answering. I consider calling my son to hear his voice but know I can't take the risk; he might pick up on my anxiety.

I spend more time agonising, then head back to the venue. I'm so tense, I get into an argument with the local promoter who's pissed that I'm not doing an interval (the venue loses money on drinks sales so he has to pay them extra) and wants to sell drinks from the bar throughout the concert instead. And I tell him no because, well fuck, the bar is at the back of the hall, in the same room as the piano, and I don't want people rummaging around for change and asking for a Heineken during the adagio of a Beethoven sonata. I think it's great that people can come to a concert of mine and have a drink while I'm playing, but not if they're getting up in the middle and chatting to the barman. He doesn't get it. But after a quick phone call with my team it's sorted, although he doesn't speak a word to me for the rest of the evening.

On stage, I'm aware of a voice in my head telling me, ordering me, that I will *not* let the aggressive text messages about the 'parking ticket' ruin the gig. For once it is on my side, trying to help me out. God, how I wish I knew how to summon that voice at will. It's reminding me that the world is a big, adventurous, wonderful place filled with people experiencing things I cannot even imagine, both good and bad. That big, lovely things are coming my way – the radio shows, the studio recording and, most importantly, my boy's visit at Christmas (my first Christmas with him in years and something I'm so insanely excited about I can barely breathe when thinking about it) – and to crumble now would let the bad win, and that is simply not an option. I dig deep because that better part of me knows how true this is. Somehow, somewhere, I find this reservoir of energy and strength that turns off the worry, the anger and the panic and, *Matrix*-style, I disappear down the rabbit hole and find myself in the oasis that is music.

I want to steal the piano, it's so wonderful. The sound is rich and full, the notes have just the right amount of depth and weight to them, the tone is like centuries-old polished mahogany. The audience is once again quiet and focused and it's such a joy. When that happens and it really feels like everyone is there, really present, it's as if we're all sharing something unique. A moment in time that will never be repeated.

This time, it's the Beethoven sonata that scratches my inner itch and helps me through. This piece is something else. It has the whole lot – the innocent simplicity of the opening movement where, like kids lying on the damp grass looking up at the stars in the sky and asking all the big questions (will I fall in love, is there a God, who are we going to miss more: Bowie or Prince), there's a sense of gentleness, understanding and purity. What is completely astonishing is that almost the entire thematic material for the whole sonata can be found compressed into the opening two bars of this piece. It is so concentrated, taut, intense, that those opening two bars contain within them the theme of the last movement, parts of the second movement and almost all of the opening movement material. It's a kind of miracle: something huge, powerful and complex emerging entirely out of seemingly nothing but those ten seconds of music. This is Beethoven turning water into wine through music.

And then, after the six-minute opening movement, comes a short, two-minute scherzo second movement. It's a question-and-answer routine, filled with dialogue, a musical argument – he asks the question quietly and then the answer is shouted at us. He throws in a couple of references to a German drinking song for good measure (amusingly titled 'I'm a Bum, You're a Bum'). Which seems so out of place but yet provides a magnificent contrast between the heavenly beauty of the rest of the sonata and the raucous, jarring ugliness of this movement. As if he's reminding us there is room for all of it here in the vastness of creative energy he's giving us – beauty and ugliness happily coexisting. Just like (and forgive the stretch here, but

Ludwig, just like Bach, did talk and write about God a lot) Jesus made it clear that even the lowliest deserve a place in heaven. That our minds and our world can be filled with both good and bad, and the whole is still amazing.

There is a really tricky page in this movement – the right hand has to move down from the top to the bottom of the keyboard playing super-fast while the left hand hits a succession of awkwardly spaced notes in the opposite direction – from the bottom of the keyboard, the middle, then crossing over the right hand (which is still motoring along at pace) to hit notes at the top. There's so much that can go wrong here. The coordination is challenging, the speed alarming, constant abrupt changes in volume; the potential to miss one note and then have the whole thing come falling down like a house of cards is enormous. But that's the thrill of pieces like this, especially live. You can play it safe, go nice and slow and measured or, as I choose to do, perhaps rashly, let go and let rip and take off at the speed that feels right, if slightly terrifying. It comes good 70 per cent of the time, but that number is increasing the more I perform it.

But then after the scherzo we get the real magic: the immense final movement. Beethoven completely ignores the rules and what's expected of him in this sonata. It's his thirty-first of thirty-two piano sonatas (what have *you* done today?) and by now he's close to the end of his life and in full-on revolutionary, fuck-da-police mode. It starts with a slow introduction, a bit like a recitative in opera – a short couple of minutes setting us up for what is going to be the most profound expression of sorrow in all of his sonatas. There are some really strange moments in this piece. One minute in, there is a single A, high up, struck and then repeated nearly thirty times, giving us the impression that time simply doesn't exist any more. There is a complete lack of melodic or harmonic movement here; it's a twilight zone, a semi-religious trance-like state.

There are odd harmonic progressions – it starts in B flat minor but gets to A flat minor via E major within a few bars (non-musicians, just trust me when I say that's odd, a bit like a movie switching both genres and actors seamlessly and unexpectedly while somehow not causing any kind of disconnect with the viewer). And then this heartbreaking melody emerges, singing out over a constantly beating left-hand accompaniment, all the fight knocked out of him. It gradually subsides, resigned in its sadness. Beethoven called it his 'Song of Lamentation'. The theme music to my last couple of days.

Then from bleakness and desperation to the first chink of light and hope in a while: Beethoven writes a fugue. And with it, the possibility of the resurrection of the human spirit when faced with so much tragedy and despair. A fugue is similar to singing 'rounds' at school. A beautiful, gentle, simple melody starting alone then continuing on its journey as an identical melody appears on top of it and starts to chase it, both of these melodies (or 'voices') proceeding on their way while yet another, third identical voice joins in underneath, until three of the same melodies are happening all at once, staggered in time but harmonically fitting like an incredibly complex, beautiful jigsaw puzzle. It builds and builds, the volume ebbing and flowing, the tension coming and going, light battling darkness, the darkness overcoming and winning before exploding, changing key again from major to minor and plummeting back into the depths of despair.

At this point in the score, Beethoven writes 'exhausted' over the notes. He is shattered with grief and won't let us escape it just yet. This is his musical depiction of his own deeply personal crisis, and it ain't over. The previous devastatingly sad melody returns, slightly adapted and ornamented to make it even more searching and bleak. At this point we can even hear Beethoven struggling to breathe in the music – he writes his sighs and gasps into the melody, using musical slurs to portray inhaling, exhaling and gasping, conveying through music the fact that he's so overwhelmed with sadness he is gasping for air. This is like reading his diaries it is so intimate.

It subsides once again until he pulls off an absolute master-stroke of genius. Just as we are expecting it to end as it did the last time – dying away into nothingness, resolving in its original key and ready for the fugue to start – he switches things around and instead of landing on a minor key (something we've been expecting for ages given the harmonic structure and what's come before) he does the musical equivalent of a massive plot twist and, after an almost unbearable moment of silence, lands on a super quiet *major* chord which he then slowly repeats ten times – ten thudding, slow heartbeats, gradually getting louder and louder, as loud as you can play, the pedal held down the whole time until there is just this immense wall of sound hurled out and filling the air (perhaps signifying the death of Christ – there is so much religious symbolism in this piece). The pedal still down, the sound still huge, he gives us a run of notes, very slowly, from the very bottom of the keyboard, starting loudly but getting quieter and quieter, disappearing into the already diminishing sound cloud hanging in the air and then, as if by magic, as the sound dissipates over time, the fugue we heard earlier emerges quietly out of the ether from up on high, alone, fragile, reawakened.

Except this time he inverts it – he takes the same melody as the previous fugue subject but he turns it upside down (like he's placed the score in front of a mirror), and puts it in G major. I know this is technical and won't mean much to you but you cannot imagine the balls of this guy – moving from B flat minor to A flat minor to A flat major to G flat major to G minor to G major and then somehow back to A flat major is fucking insane; it's like writing a play with the final act first and the opening act last and some speeches delivered backwards. But it all somehow makes sense – it is a masterpiece in harmony, development and innovation. The net effect is that we recognise this fugue subject but aren't really sure how or why we do: musical déjà vu. It's so impossibly fragile, like it could break at any moment, this magical melody that has appeared out of this wall of sound as if descending from the heavens. It starts to get more complicated, fuller, bigger, braver, louder, faster, as he begins the process of untangling it and turning it back the right way up, until in a final blaze of glory we explode, loudly, heroically, back to the original fugue subject and key, the melody getting higher and higher up the keyboard, raising himself up to the heavens and searching desperately for salvation until it arrives in one final, epic, huge terrific cascade of beauty, plummeting from the top of the keyboard to the bottom and back up again.

It is twenty-two minutes that lasts a lifetime and contains

a lifetime. It is his biopic. It is everything that is good in the universe.

The audience in Berlin remains completely silent throughout the whole thing. I mean, not a peep. Not a cough, a rustle, a movement. I feel, possibly for the first time in my life, that were Beethoven alive today and there in that room (and had a really tip-top hearing aid), he wouldn't have been completely appalled. He might have actually felt inclined to high-five me after.

Whenever I play this particular sonata by Beethoven I can't help but share those feelings he carried with him. It's as if they were trapped inside him, and writing them out as a series of musical notes was the only way he knew to exorcise them. While I can't even begin to express them on paper like he did, playing Op. 110 comes a close second. This evening that sonata in particular seems to scrape out all my inner shit in a way that renders words useless and relies instead on the magic of music to do the seemingly impossible. The entire cycle of emotions contained in it seems to replicate what's going on in my head and heart on repeat throughout each twenty-four hours. The moments of optimism and gentleness of the opening where there are hints of something darker and heavier to come. The recklessness of the scherzo. And, of course, the intense journey of the final movement. The exhaustion, unbearable sadness, glimpses of hope, the effort spent trying to unearth and sustain that hope – trying, failing, failing better.

It is the most aspirational piece of music I know.

I end up giving six encores (a record for me).

You'd think that would be more than enough to see me through, at least until the following morning. But then, back at the hotel, things start to go wrong. Playing and getting lost in that sonata, combined with so little sleep, has stirred things up deep down. I'm feeling raw and exposed.

I eat. In the room. Alone. As per usual. All of those damaging thoughts and voices that I somehow managed to push down or distract myself from on stage are coming at me with machetes. This time I just can't control it. Not even using my look-out-for-that-thought exercise that used to work so well. I'm exhausted, wired and desperate for sleep but I can't do it. There is such a rage building up. I'd managed to bury the feelings arising from those text messages from earlier, but now, in the distraction-free safety of my hotel room, the disappointment has turned into fury which has morphed into a Rottweiler, its jaws around my throat, refusing to let me go. I can't ever remember feeling so angry, so powerless, so misunderstood and invisible. At least not since I was a kid. Which is probably what's really behind this.

Every hour or so I get out of bed, giving up on chasing sleep, walk down to the entrance to smoke yet another cigarette. No one is picking up their phones (it's approaching 5 a.m. again so no surprise there) and I am alone with it. It's made worse knowing that I have a concert in Dresden later that day. The pressure of knowing I have to get some sleep, the feelings of rage and impotence, the adrenalin spike from the previous night's concert and the anger all combine, and I don't sleep all night. The urge to email or call the person who issued the ticket is overwhelming, but I have learned one thing (possibly only one thing) over the past few years which is never, ever, ever to send a message at 3 a.m. about an emotive topic. And I don't. Which is the one decent thing I manage to achieve that whole night.

I doze in the car to Dresden and put my faith in the on-stage adrenalin to carry me through that night's gig. There's no other choice. It works. Another focused, quiet audience, a beautiful Steinway Model D (the best there is, something I'll keep repeating shamelessly in this book on the off chance they'll give me one for free), three encores, books signed.

After the gig I finally get hold of my shrink. We have a long chat and together we write an email to the council about the 'parking ticket'. It explains the giant gap in reality between the incident itself and the fine they are imposing and simply asks them to reflect on that. It's kind and restrained but also firm, and establishes some boundaries. There's no judgement in it and no blame. There's no self-pity or manipulation. As I hit send I feel something let go.

Room service dinner (the same thing I had for lunch – if it ain't broke . . .) and finally after a few days of too little sleep I pass out by midnight, my body doing for me what my mind cannot do for itself.

I wake up feeling more settled. One final gig tonight before I get to return to London for a week. Munich. It's a long drive. Nearly five hours. Five and a half with cigarette and bratwurst stops. But when we arrive I have plenty of time. They've gone all out on this occasion and got me a junior suite at a lovely hotel. Perhaps because it's the last night of the current leg of the tour. It feels so luxurious. Room to spread out a little, watch some TV, eat at a table rather than on a bed.

I'm playing in the Carl-Orff-Saal. Which is really, really grown up. It's in the same building as the Berliner Philharmonie and there are posters everywhere of von Karajan and Furtwängler and other conducting titans. This is the first properly 'classical' hall I've played in so far, the rest being mainly theatres. My head immediately switches into 'fraud mode'. This 'imposter syndrome' thing has been a regular thing for years. I understand it's quite common in creative people and those in positions of authority. As well as in complete phonies like me. I don't belong here, this is where the grown-ups play, there's bound to be press coming, I'm so fucked. You know the score by now.

But this time, it turns out, I can handle it. Either the worst is over, or perhaps I'm just too tired to care any more. I tell myself I'm supposed to enjoy this, I want to enjoy this. I'm performing in one of the major concert halls in Europe, playing music that I've carried with me for so many years and that has saved my ass more times than I care to remember. I'm being paid to do this. People are paying to come and see me do it. I have a manager, tour manager, German promoter, local promoter, UK promoter, German publishing house, UK publishers all working together to make this tour a success and, equally importantly, I've got a bunch of really lovely German fans, many of whom are waiting armed with photos and sharpies at the stage door when I arrive, and who for some reason, inexplicable or not, want to see me play and hear me talk. I tell that part of myself that's always trying to trip me up and gets hard out of making me feel out of place, to go fuck itself.

I walk onto the stage, bow, sit and pause and start that opening arpeggio of the Bach C major prelude. And as I hit those first few notes I know I'm going to be just fine.

AFFIRMATION 5:

'When I align myself with
a loving Higher Power,
I happily accept everything that
life gives me.'

TRANSLATION:

'I AM CAPABLE OF ACCEPTING THAT SHIT HAPPENS.
SOMETIMES.'

CONCERT PIECE NUMBER FIVE

Rachmaninov Prelude Op. 32/13

Sergei Rachmaninov, once referred to as a 'six-and-a-half-foot scowl' (although taking the piss out of him for being bipolar doesn't seem particularly kind), is another one of my TTHs™.

The guy chose, bravely, to stick to his guns when it came to tonality, seeing himself as much less concerned with pushing harmonic boundaries than his contemporaries Schoenberg, Hindemith or Stravinsky. He liked to say his music was in the genre 'of flowing, lush effects and illuminated vistas viewed from a romantic point'. He wanted to engulf the listener in warmth and to transport them to an ideal planet, even if, as he acknowledged, there was an almost constant undercurrent of sadness in his works. He spoke of the culmination point that can be found in all of his compositions, sometimes in the middle, sometimes at the end, but that always 'this moment must arrive with the sound and sparkle of a ribbon snapped at the end of a race – it must seem like a liberation from the last material object, the last barrier between truth and its expression'. His music always breaks through that barrier.

His Prelude Op. 32/13 is a symphony in five minutes, far, far greater than the sum of its individual parts. It is based on the simplest of themes – just three notes, a D flat major arpeggio – F, A flat, D flat. The entire thing is based on those three notes. But every time they are played they are followed by a loud, usually discordant octave that constantly interrupts such a joyful, flowing, unassuming little melody. Sergei was so brave, so willing to expose his innermost thoughts, feelings and fears in his music. He showed us what was in his heart, no matter how ugly or scary that was. He wrote once that 'when writing down my music, [I try] to make it say simply and directly that which is in my heart'. It's musical bipolar disorder – Rachmaninov's depression laid bare in front of us and the constant, daily struggle between the two voices of good and evil inside our (his, my) heads. These two voices go to war during the piece. It gets progressively more and more violent, angular, unsettled until it's a full-on battle, and it's not until the very end, after thousands of notes and a lot of sweat, that the good voice wins.

It is the most triumphant ending, filled with cascading octaves and chords so huge that it is physically impossible to play them as written with just two hands. You need to split them, playing the main chord and the underlying notes as close to the same time as possible and finding a tiny microsecond to jump from one to the other so as to fit all the notes in. It's a struggle both physically and emotionally and feels as if, without sounding too grandiose, one has to beat the piano into submission.

In many ways, it is a perfect allegory of the past few months for me. There is beauty and good which is constantly being harangued, assaulted and doubted by a voice seemingly beyond any human control. They kick and fight until finally, exhausted, the good defeats the bad, *Star Wars*-style, and there is shining, redemptive acceptance and victory ringing out. I'm not quite there yet, I'm still in the kicking and fighting bit of the story – one of the lightsabre battles. The darkness in this piece is very dark indeed – some extraordinary key changes, a chromaticism (where the notes don't fit in with the composition's diatonic scale) that is almost unbearable, a torrid, raging, out-of-control kind of madness that threatens to go completely off the rails but is dragged and wrestled back down to where it belongs through sheer muscle. Rachmaninov is shouting a giant 'fuck you' at the top of his voice to that part of him that wants him dead. I'm trying to do the same thing. And I'm feeling hopeful.

*

LONDON, OCTOBER 2016

I feel as if I might be changing. In a good way.

After Dresden I fly back to London for a miraculously quiet stretch of time before I head back to Germany and Austria for seven more concerts in seven different cities in nine days.

I know I've changed because as I arrive home and walk through my front door, all the anger disappears and I have a moment of utter clarity where I realise how ridiculous the whole 'parking ticket' situation is.

The problem is that although losing the car was definitely for the best, the car was, at least at times, like my best friend.

It had its quirks, but we went on some lovely journeys together and forged some memories I'll treasure.

I want to find a way to say goodbye properly, or else I worry it will consume me to the point that I won't recover from it and I will just be bitter and resentful for years. It's a risk because I've no idea how it will unfold. I just know it's more likely to be better than it is at the moment.

Somehow, I find the courage, or idiocy, to call and arrange a face-to-face meeting. And, by a stroke of dumb luck and lots of deep breaths, I manage to achieve some kind of closure over a cup of tea. The anger dissolves and I drop the sense of betrayal. It sets me free and allows me that much-needed, humane goodbye.

I know, deep down, that it's done now.

For the first time in my life I am ready and willing to face the fact that this chapter of my life is truly over, and that I'd better start tolerating, or even enjoying, my own company because when it comes down to it, that's all I have. Glenn Gould once told an interviewer in 1966 that live audiences were a 'force of evil' because pleasing them took precedence over his pursuit of perfection. 'I really thank God that I'm able to sit in a studio with enormous concentration and do things many times, if necessary,' he said. While I love performing live, I feel the exact same way about the sanctity, freedom and privacy of the recording studio. I hope you'll forgive the stretch here, but it feels as if my world has become a metaphoric version of Gould's safe and protected recording studio where a whole new realm has opened up for me, and having that sense of space and freedom has liberated me from the audience I'd spent so much energy and time trying to please at such immense cost. It has, if I don't fuck it up, the potential to allow me to be me. The real me. Finally.

I figure baby steps are needed to start me off. I decide to make my flat more liveable-in. It's small and pretty sparse, with cheap and functional furniture from IKEA. I walk into town to visit my friend Matthew, and he and I take his new baby, my goddaughter, for a walk and head down to Tottenham Court Road. Matthew is extraordinary. Despite the normal ups and downs of life, he doesn't seem to let it get to him. At least not visibly. He struggles appropriately and doesn't buckle or collapse. He's been happily married for ages, he has two perfect children, an amazing wife, a good, responsible job and a calm reassuring voice whenever I need it. I am in awe of him. There are perhaps, on a really good day, three people in this world who I trust. He's top of that list.

Once he told me he had had a 'terrible argument' with his wife. 'One of the worst ever,' he said morosely. I started thinking of arguments I'd had with exes. The vile things said, bile and scorn pouring out of our mouths, words that could never be taken back, objects thrown. I'm worried, so I say to him, 'God, bro, I am so sorry. Is everything OK? What happened?' And he looks pained and says to me, 'For the first time ever, I actually had to say to her "I don't feel like I'm being heard."' That was it. No raised voices, no swearing, no negative sexual comparisons with previous lovers, no violence of any kind. Just a calm statement of fact.

Oh, and his job involves him saving lives on a daily basis.

So it does me good to be around him.

We head to furniture shops where I order a small dining table that can be folded down (eating on the sofa in front of the TV each night isn't such a good idea, psychologically), some chairs, a new coffee table, a lovely, soft rug for the bare floor of my living room, and some storage shelves. Matty is in his element. He loves this shit. Me, I glaze over and just want to get it done; I would have preferred to order it all online and with no human interaction. But he's a stable influence, as I said, and in person it actually doesn't feel so bad. In a couple of weeks I'll have, to all intents and purposes, an entirely new flat. It'll be warm and snug. If our outer worlds tend to match our inner ones then I'm going to feel much better.

I think perhaps that self-esteem comes only from doing estimable things. No one can give it to me. Sadly. It has to be built up gradually and, annoyingly, it's becoming more and more apparent that the only way I can get through this life with some semblance of a smile is to start to feel some love and compassion for myself. Two things I've run from as much as possible. But it feels like I've run out of time now. It's make or break – either start to be a little gentler with myself or disintegrate. I've tried marriage. I've tried money, sex, food, drugs, alcohol, self-harm, anything and everything to escape, and it's all stopped working. I've tried Trimipramine, Quetiapine, Mirtazapine, Effexor, Citalopram, Escitalopram, Venlafaxine, Sulpiride, Clonazepam, Olanzapine, Fluoxetine, Pregabalin, Paroxetine, Risperidone, Alprazolam, Diazepam, Lorazepam, heroin, coke, LSD, pot, speed, ecstasy, whisky, gin, wine, beer and countless other substances. All to no avail, other than temporary, and incredible, numbness. The only choice left open to me now is to properly recover in a very human way (complete with flaws and slip-ups) or to carry on trying to keep my head above water by distracting myself with things that aren't good for me.

Baby steps turn into toddler ones. I go food shopping and fill the fridge and freezer with healthy stuff so that I don't starve or eat takeaway shit. I carry on going for long walks. I book myself into a few yoga classes. Yoga. Me. But it's awesome. I find a version I'd never heard of called yin yoga which is basically slow-motion yoga. You go into various poses and hold them for four, five or six minutes. It's painful at first. Most of the poses are designed to open up the hips, and my whole pelvic/hip area is a fucking wasteland. There's been so much physical damage done from when I was a kid that the ligaments, bones and muscles are all messed up and the general area looks like a hand grenade has gone off in there.

I've also got these titanium rods in my spine to help keep me upright after my lower disc exploded from the physical trauma of being raped, and so there's a lot of hard, gnarly scar tissue there as well which doesn't help things. So these slow poses are heavy for me emotionally as well as physically. They release so much emotion – the body never, ever forgets. Memories and feelings are stored in there as reliably as data on a hard drive, always ready to be recalled with the click of a mouse or the right password. And yin is the password that opens things up for me. It takes me completely by surprise but I spend every session crying quietly in the corner as feelings flow from down there. I can't help it.

My sleeping starts to improve too. There's something that I discovered during a yoga class that really helps me at night. If you can ignore the ridiculous vocabulary and awful New Age condescension of most teachers, yoga is a seriously beneficial tool. This particular brand is called yoga nidra (which, as you all know, means yogic sleep in Sanskrit). It's that weird, twilight zone in between waking and sleeping, and is a kind of meditation that allows us to enter that state where we are increasingly aware of that inner world. It's basically the deepest state of relaxation you can get while still being fully conscious. It's been used to treat PTSD in soldiers with some success. It's unbelievably helpful to me.

You lie down (an immediate bonus) and bring your attention to various parts of your body in a specific order. You do not move, just keep your eyes closed, and especially do not move the parts of your body you're placing your awareness on, just feel the energy there. You start with the right thumb and move through all your fingers, then right wrist, forearm, elbow, upper arm, armpit, down to the right side of the torso, into the right hip, thigh, knee, lower leg, ankle, sole of foot, top of foot and toes. It's amazing how quickly specific areas start to feel as if they're tingling, alive and energised.

You then do the same with the left side. Then move from your lower back up to the middle and upper back and shoulders, then the base of the spine up to the base of the neck, the neck itself, back of the head, top of the head, forehead, eyes, ears, cheeks, nose, mouth, tongue, jaw, throat, right collar bone, left collar bone, middle of the chest, down into the stomach and finally the solar plexus. Spending about fifteen seconds on each part and breathing gently and deeply as you do it.

Once you've gone through all these bits you then feel the entire torso at once, the arms and legs at once, the head and torso together and finally the whole body. You experience the inner energy of your entire being and, more often than not, by this point you're either fast asleep or practically levitating. Either one is a good result for me.

I started doing this every night before bed. Although my sleep is still hyper-irregular, what it's done is bring me back into my body, which is a place I'd run from all my life. When the abuse was happening I would always leave my body, fly out of it and far away (flying is still my favourite childhood memory, which partly explains the raging drug use in my teenage years as I tried desperately to recreate that feeling).

Ever since then it's been very hard to come back to it. For example, I get confused about certain body parts still, calling elbows knees and ankles wrists, and it takes a while sometimes to really know what part is where. I know how backwards that sounds. But as a kid I simply had to distance myself from my own body because it was just too dangerous and painful to inhabit it. And it's evidently taking me a long time to work my way back to myself.

But this yoga nidra helps. Somehow just getting back in touch with that inner energy has had a profound impact on every level. I get to experience the elusive inner world that I so love about Beethoven and that he was forced into due to his deafness. That state of interiority that is so prevalent in his music. It boosts the immune system, helps me feel more grounded, allows me the space and sense of safety to lean into challenging feelings, helps me to feel tranquil and quiet, even if only for an hour. Stillness is one of the greatest gifts of meditation and yoga. I'm a guy who cannot be still. Who paces, twitches, thinks, fidgets, expends energy all the time, even ostensibly for no reason. Stillness is something I need a lot more of.

Imagine a world where this kind of thing is taught in schools. It would be the beginning of the end of the anxiety epidemic. I'm pretty sure that within a generation or two, conflict and war would rapidly become the exception rather than the daily reality and prescriptions for anxiety would be slashed dramatically.

So my days, my life in between concerts, are filled with nesting and nurturing. Perhaps I needed to wait to be truly alone before doing this. There are whole days where it's just me, my yoga, my piano and my thoughts. I'm slowly coming face to face with it all. What's amazing is that I'm staying with it, as best I can.

The universe looks like it's meeting me halfway when, one day during that week in London, a pre-release recording of Currentzis's new disc of *Don Giovanni* lands in my hallway. <Teenage-girl-diary number of exclamation marks>

It arrives from Sony, couriered over because I'd hassled them all for so long about it they just wanted me out of their inboxes, and I sit late into the evening, marvelling at yet another miracle from the Greek-Russian conductor. It is, unbelievably, even better than *Figaro* and *Così fan tutte*. The orchestra does things, makes sounds that I've never heard before. The singers are transported from decent, semi well-known opera singers into Callas rivals; the depth of Mozart's genius is there in all of its magnificence and carries me away in a wave of ecstasy. I spend hours and hours in my newly comfy flat, listening to it.

This one is about a young, arrogant nobleman (think Donald Trump in the 1980s) who fucks, rapes and murders his way around town, abuses and pisses off everyone else in the cast until he encounters something he cannot kill, beat up, dodge, or outwit – a giant statue called the *Commendatore*, the murdered father of a girl Don Giovanni tried to rape. Giovanni killed him in a duel following the attack. He then makes a move on another woman he passes in the street after the attack. And *then*, dick presumably almost falling off, goes on to try and shag a woman on her wedding day. He's classy like that. His manservant's best aria is all about his boss the Don shagging 1,003 different women. Which, pre-Tinder, is quite a figure.

It's a hell of an opera. Mozart uses trombones to represent this statue towards the end of the opera which would've made his audience shit themselves because in his day *no one* used trombones other than in church. By the end, we are almost in Hitchcock territory. It's terrifying. Full of dissonant sevenths and insane tension as the Don refuses to repent despite the *Commendatore*'s ghost urging him to and giving him one last chance or face being consigned to hell for evermore, but it's too late. Giovanni tells the whole world to go fuck itself and maintains unapologetically that he can do whatever he wants (hello again, Donald), that pleasure and free will are the most important things. The Don dies and is dragged down to hell. This is the high point of the entire opera – the message laid bare for us all to learn from and an absolute climax filled with horror, damnation and hell.

Yet at the exact point where he is dragged down into the inferno, as the entire cast screams in terror witnessing the horrors of hell and damnation, the audience on the edge of their seats, the music at its apex, Da Ponte, who wrote the lyrics, goes full-on anti-Hollywood and just gives the perfectly simple, slightly laconic stage direction:

'Fire on all sides; earthquake.'

Which is kind of the epitome of understatement, and also a pretty perfect description of how I feel about my life the majority of the time. There is fire on all sides and an earthquake starting to rumble. It's hot and dangerous and my world is either about to melt or collapse.

Exquisitely, rather than end it there where perhaps it would be most natural, Mozart, with his giant fucking heart, gives us a finale filled with a sense of joy, wonder and transformation as the rest of the cast delights in Don Giovanni's disappearance and the music moves into the major key with melody after melody nailing us to the back of our chairs, this time in delight rather than terror. The fire has been extinguished, the earthquake avoided.

Listening to it reinforces the growing belief in me that, although I don't think I need to repent for what happened to me as a kid, or indeed for trying to sleep with loads of women (albeit usually unsuccessfully and certainly an awful lot fewer than the Don), I really do need to work even harder at changing my life, to stop allowing my mind to dictate the direction it's taking and contaminate everything good with its toxic fucking voice.

There are so many things I need to do now, to put into practice. Start trusting people, for example. Not everyone perhaps, but certainly my core group. Start believing in the goodness in people and in the world. Start ignoring the constant stream of invective and lies my head tells me about everything. Start taking care of myself – eating, sleeping, exercising. Start believing in myself a little bit more, finding some sense of compassion for myself and, in particular, the child I was. Start forgiving myself for fucking up countless relationships. Start recognising and acknowledging the many small acts I am now doing each day that help build myself back up. Not the big gestures like giving to charity so I can feel good about myself, but more the anonymous, humble little things and small acts of kindness to myself and others that really count.

An ex-girlfriend said to me a while ago that it wasn't the lovely presents and luxury hotels that made things special during our relationship; it was the occasional random notes I'd leave for her telling her I loved her. Perhaps with a stick man drawing (me) with a giant penis (me being ironic) and a couple of lines about how I missed her or some heartfelt Rumi (TTH™) quote. Simple little scraps of paper with kind thoughts left for her to find when she got home from work were what made her feel loved and cherished. While all the time I believed that if I didn't lavish attention and expense on partners they'd up and leave, because without that, what did they have? Nothing, other than me. And that wasn't anything like good enough. I had to compensate them for choosing to be with me.

I find that desperately sad. The core, unquestioned belief that on my own, as I am, I am so far from good enough that I have to buy love. Or at least bribe it. And sadder still, like so many of us who feel the same way, I was perhaps completely wrong. All this time I've operated from a single, erroneous assumption – I am worthless. What if, in fact, my exes just really fucking loved me, found me hot and charming and occasionally funny and just wanted me as I am? That they stayed with me *despite* the things I felt I needed to do to keep them, not because of those things? Holy shit. Imagine that for a minute. That would change everything. Like discovering the world was indeed round rather than flat. That maybe it wasn't fire on all sides at all. It was just a lovely, warm breeze.

Funnily enough, a few days before the second half of the Germany tour, I meet another girl. I promise I wasn't looking for it. I'd been adamant that I'd wait until I had sorted myself out, right? If anything, of late it had felt like my libido had just died of a heart attack suddenly. No urge to have sex whatsoever. But here I am, smoking outside my yoga studio (feeling slightly ashamed) after a class, and this girl comes out and gives me a look that's a cross between contempt – she's clearly slightly appalled by the Marlboros – and admiration.

We start talking and I offer her a smoke, just to rile her up a bit, which she declines. She is really pretty. A thirty-year-old Naomi Watts lookalike. But most beautiful is the energy she has. It's coming off her in waves, just absolute visceral openness, joy, ecstasy and wonder. She's so open, so present, I feel like she sees everything and there's nowhere to hide and I want to bathe in whatever it is she's giving off. Or maybe I'm just really Zenned out from yoga.

After chatting for a bit, I ask her out for a coffee and off we go (yay) and talk. For hours. When she's looking at me I'm the only person in the café and I choose my words carefully because she's actually listening and aware. I swear she's like some weird angel. With an awesome accent – a mixture of Australian, South African, Spanish – a legacy of years of travelling and working abroad.

After a while it's getting too much. I feel like I'm drowning in something lovely, but it's too overwhelming. I bolt. Politely but quickly. Too many feels. But walking home I can't stop thinking about her. I'm pissed off I didn't get her number or give her mine and I've never seen her at yoga before so there's no guarantee I'll see her again. And I want to. Because it felt like she was kind, slightly zany, happy to move towards things rather than shutting down and pushing things away. Even if it doesn't turn into anything intimate, I realise that I'm in desperate need of someone like this in my life. In retrospect I was, perhaps, still so lonely and doing my favourite trick of imbuing perfectly nice, ordinary people with magical qualities.

I get home still thinking about this girl, Clara. I sleep straight through for the first time in weeks.

The next morning, I wake up and do my usual morning routine – 100 press-ups, 100 sit-ups, 5k jog, home for a shower, followed by a 30-minute meditation. I make organic porridge with water and goji berries, sit quietly and eat breakfast in silence, enjoying the contemplation.

Yep. Maybe one day.

I fall out of bed, dressing gown on, stumble to the kitchen, kettle on, bathroom for the best wee of the day, radio on, back to kitchen, make tea (decaf, lots of milk, no sugar), light up the first (and most gratifying) cigarette of the day, check my phone. And amidst the dozens of emails, most of which are totally ignorable, there's a notification telling me someone wants to send me a message on Instagram. I click on it to see who it is and it's Clara. She's found me. I respond and we swap numbers and arrange to go for a walk later that day.

We meet and it's like two best friends realigning with one

another after a few years apart. Very, very quickly we're back in step with each other. I know this is an opportunity to practise what I'm learning. It's never going to be anything serious, but it could be a chance to prepare for the real thing when and if that ever comes along at some point in the future. It's relationship homework. There is no deceit, I tell her no lies, we don't ask difficult questions of one another; it is simply enjoyable, present companionship.

Even better, I'm practising not pretending to be anyone other than me, as I had promised myself. One of the legacies of the past few weeks and months is that I've made a commitment to stop trying to be whoever I think other people wanted me to be. With the actress it was Person A (confident/ secure), with my ex-wives Person C (funny/charming) and D (vulnerable) with a bit of E (introvert) thrown in. With Denis it's Person B (extrovert) with a smattering of F (shy/humble). On stage it's a combination of them all. They are made up of fragments of the whole but can never be the whole itself. There is an underlying belief that Person Zero, who I really am, with all of my faults and quirks, just cannot be enough, has to be supplemented and augmented by other facets. I'm sure we all do this to some extent, but I've ended up building a succession of personalities, some intentional, others entirely subconscious and uncontrollable (the ones that have been with me since childhood, that arrived to help keep me upright as my mind fractured and broke). Keeping track of all of them is hard and exhausting, and when I also have an unconscious, automatic system in place that substitutes personalities depending on the situation I find myself in, then it becomes even more challenging. And so, enough now. I am resolved to be me, even if it means people don't like that.

I know that seeing Clara and exploring where this might go is against everything that I've agreed with myself: to have space, to just be with me for a while, to learn to enjoy being alone and then be able to come to a relationship from a place of not needing to be with someone simply because I can't handle being alone. But even my shrink tells me I'm not great on my own. So I think, 'fuck it'. As we walk, talk, drink tea and go to bed, I tell myself this is better than being alone, surely.

She seems to be so open, so secure, so free. With a boundless energy that is infectious. And she really, really likes me (a new experience for me). In bed she is completely liberated – happy to tell me what she likes and doesn't like, completely comfortable in her own, naked, soft skin. That is also something of a first for me. There is a complete absence of shame, guilt or awkwardness (the three things I feel the most when naked with someone else). I realise that perhaps this is a wonderful opportunity thrown my way to explore that side of things. To learn to be more open. Clara is heavily into tantra and sexological bodywork (I laughed out loud when she told me, but it is apparently a real thing); she had studied it and worked with it for a long time. It's remarkable. There is this weird and wonderful fusing of energies and a feeling of safety and easiness that I have never experienced before. At least this is what I tell her.

Honestly, it's just fucking great to do fun things with my wiener. Tantra, shmantra. She's super sweet, but I'm beginning to think that, like me, she's caught a little bit (perhaps even quite a lot) of crazy at some point in her life. Still, it makes for a pleasant distraction. The shallow me decides to go with it.

A deeper part of me is thinking I'm rushing head-on into a massive car crash. But it's outvoted by the committee (and my wiener). I figure, worst case, we have a few weeks of fun and then we go our separate ways. And that can't be a bad thing.

I am the master at self-justification.

Here I go again – two doors in front of me, one marked 'Idiot: What Are You Thinking?' the other marked 'A Chance for Peace', and I'm straight through the former without a backward glance. While whistling. Because of course even if it's just a fling it's still taking up energy and head space, making noise, causing ripples and waves and moving me away from where I'd promised myself I'd move towards just a few days before. There is still, it seems, this unavoidable pull towards drama and pain because that is my default setting, and even that is better than being alone with myself with no distractions.

GERMANY TOUR PART 2
(incl. Switzerland and Austria)

The next day I'm at Heathrow. Again. Heading to Frankfurt for the second half of the Germany tour. Seven concerts in seven cities in nine days. It's full on. Packed with trains, planes, automobiles and Steinways. But as I sit in Terminal 3 waiting for my (delayed) plane I feel infinitely less depressed than the last time I was here. I feel more confident and upbeat: these changes I've been working on are starting to consolidate and take effect. This is how I always wanted things to feel – energised and excited about touring and performing in a sustainable way, butterflies rather than panic around the girl I'm dating, a feeling of serenity and joy, mixed with a few inevitable and appropriate nerves. As I'm sitting there, aching for a cigarette but making do with a bacon sandwich, Clara texts me and says 'I don't want to intrude but whenever I've been travelling and come home I really, really love it when someone is there to meet me. What do you think? Could I come meet you at the airport the day you fly home?'

I say yes, please. I glide onto the plane feeling two stone lighter and giddy with the most beautiful feelings.

Still walking through the idiot door.

I land an hour later in Frankfurt and the German tour manager for this part is there. He has a cold which does my head in completely as I'm already feeling that I've got a bit of a bug (something has been going around in London and I simply cannot allow myself to get sick during a tour). I try and keep my distance from him as we travel on to Mainz. I also try and accept that this fear of germs that I have isn't based on a healthy reality. I cannot open bathroom doors using my hands (have to use the sleeve of my jumper or coat or a paper towel), I can't touch anything on the tube or on trains or put my hands on any surfaces that people have touched. Falling over on a rattling tube train happens far too often. Shaking hands horrifies me. I go through at least one bottle of handwash a week. I have eighteen unopened bars of soap in my bathroom cabinet just in case I run out.

It's all for the same reason that I still feel slightly nauseous when I step on a crack on the pavement, or have to count to a certain number, or tap a certain rhythm or grunt and squeak a certain way. I know it's about control, fear and an inability to trust and let go. But it does have such a hold on me. If you operate in a certain way and reinforce certain beliefs for decades, it's going to take a while to undo.

When we arrive I check into the Hilton, dump my bags and head off to the venue, which is a ten-minute walk away.

Everything is marvellously German-efficient. The technicians get the lighting right within a few minutes and I do a quick radio interview. I'm in my green room, ready and waiting to go on stage, when I receive a few messages from Clara:

'Honey what you do is changing the world one note at a time'

'It's beyond important and crucial and beautiful'

'One note at a time, my butterfly!!'

'You might seem delicate but your butterfly wings create storms and waves'

Shut up. I know it's ridiculous. But never in my life have I experienced someone saying things like that to me (other than Denis in his own wonderful way, but that doesn't really count because he's my manager and that's his job and I don't want to hose him). It's staggering to me. Here is this stunning girl who wants to meet me at the airport, demands photos of me, actually likes the photos of me I send her, sends me the most beautiful and encouraging messages and seems to have the most open heart. All the more unexpected because I'm being as honest with her as I was with the actress, and not pulling my usual tricks like I used to.

I can't take it seriously. Even I know that. I'm still so fragile, so insanely grateful for a little bit of positive attention, and the whole tantra/New Age-y routine is too batshit even for me. I'm keeping my feet on the ground, seeing it as a short-term thing at best, with the inevitable hurt and pain, but really enjoying the fact that little moments like this can and do exist in my world now. Moments of feeling treasured, moments that I know are sincere.

The concert goes well. Not great (from my perspective) but good enough. I'm getting a bit sick (psychosomatic or otherwise) and my muscles aren't quite as agile as they could be because of that. So certain things get missed – small fluffed notes, slightly uneven runs of notes in passages that are usually fine (the arpeggios in the Beethoven aren't always even, some of the runs in the F minor *Fantasie* aren't quite as smooth as they could be). Which is frustrating. But the audience stands up at the end, and after four encores I walk down to the signing and everyone in the lobby of the theatre starts clapping. They can't all be wrong. Can they? We sell all the books and CDs, people all the while opening up to me, bringing me books and albums they think I'd like and cookies they've baked, and wanting hugs, pictures and autographs.

I get back to the hotel, shattered already, and worried because this is only the first of seven and if I'm tired now then what the fuck . . .? I order some spectacular pasta from room service and then I pass out.

Next morning, I find myself at the train station ready to go to Zürich. It's cold and I don't fancy waiting on the platform, but German trains are apparently always on time and everything is super-efficient here. Except the platform sign starts off saying it's going to be five minutes late. Which is no big deal, because one positive is that you can smoke on the platform in Germany (glorious). Then it changes to ten. In no time it's forty minutes late. It starts raining, I'm on a freezing-cold train platform, my coughing, spluttering tour manager has no idea of personal space and keeps coming close to me with germs pouring off him in waves and lunging purposefully for my mouth, I'm a walking hypochondriac and more and more anxious about missing our connecting train from Basel to Zürich. Suddenly I've turned into stress-dude.

Of course the train arrives eventually. I listen to *Don Giovanni*, close my eyes, and we arrive in Zürich where it's sunny and feels gilded by the super-wealthy who can afford to live there. A club sandwich in the three-star hotel is thirty quid. I've lost my iPhone cable so buy a new one. Forty quid. The taxi fare for a ten-minute journey – thirty-five quid. Seriously, Switzerland, what the fuck is going on with your prices? I'm suddenly grateful to live in London.

Backstage at the Theater Spirgarten there's a lot to be happy about. In my rider I usually ask for nuts, fruit, Coke (legal kind), water and Kit Kats. They've done the rest but, being Swiss, they have drawn the line at the latter. Instead there's a proud mountain of proper Swiss chocolate. Which works for me. Even better, the theatre is, oddly, connected to my hotel. So I can move from backstage to my room directly and in under thirty seconds. Which is excellent. I lie on my bed watching *Friday Night Lights* until just before show time, then head backstage. I can hear the usual pre-concert audience hubbub and instead of dread I feel excitement. This is what I've always wanted – to feel more curious than afraid. I think of all the good things. I bound on stage feeling emotionally positive (a lovely change) and play as well as I can.

Physically I still don't feel right. Like I'm getting a bit sicker and my muscles still aren't at 100 per cent. But it goes OK and the audience seems very happy. I do three encores, the last of which I'm particularly proud of. It's the Bach-Marcello Adagio. The piece of music that a friend smuggled into a psych ward for me ten years previously and had changed my life forever. It starts out as a heartbeat, a single throbbing D repeated six times before splitting into two notes and then again into four, before the melody enters and takes us down a path of pure beauty for five delicious minutes. Somehow the trills, the sound and the pedal all conspire to make this the best thing I've played in ages. At the end the audience is totally silent for a long time. No applause, no coughing, no rustling, nothing. Just letting the sound fade and the feelings linger without reality interrupting. It feels amazing.

I finish up and head to the lobby and sign a tonne of books. I meet more brilliant people, including an old school friend I haven't heard from or seen in twenty-three years but who lives in Zürich and decided to come check me out. We share some bittersweet memories (school was never my favourite place, for obvious reasons; it was all unwanted sex, alcohol, drugs, terror and exams), then I order the most expensive club sandwich in the world and eat it in my room before falling into bed.

And somehow, miraculously, sleep for ten hours.

It's my last good night's sleep in ages.

From that point onwards, everything is a bit of a jumble.

One city merges into another, airports and train stations and hotels and concert halls all become one, and all sense of place and time has gone. Hours pass in seconds, days cease to exist; jumping from Tuesdays to Fridays, I come to sporadically without knowing how I ended up wherever I am in that moment. Adrenalin, pressure, fatigue, travel – most of these things encourage dissociation.

I know I play in Hamburg. It stands out in my mind because it's a terrific concert. The best yet, actually. It's a Yamaha not a Steinway but it has a lovely sound (I always remember the piano), and when I announce that I'm going to play Rachmaninov for an encore I get a little cheer from a bunch of people and that makes my whole day. Imagine saying 'I'm going to play some Rachmaninov' and people shouting 'Yay!'. When does that ever happen, except in my dreams? What a feeling. I get a couple of very touching letters from fans afterwards. One has a Kit Kat bar attached to it, which is an added bonus (extra points because it's a chunky one). My muscles feel good that night and I'm proud of my playing, which happens probably once in every fifteen concerts. It all just feels right and I allow myself a couple of slightly bum passages without crucifying myself.

What also stands out is Vienna. Because it is there that things start going really wrong.

AFFIRMATION 6:

'Nourishing myself is a joyful experience. Abundance and love flow freely through me.'

TRANSLATION:

'YOU STUPID PRICK. JUST WHEN THINGS START TO LOOK PROMISING YOU KNOW YOU'RE ABOUT TO GET FUCKED.'

Puccini arr. Mikhashoff
'O mio babbino caro'

Everything is about love. In opera, just like in every other art form. In Puccini's *Gianni Schicchi*, the final part of his *Il trittico* ('The Triptych'), Lauretta is in love with a young guy called Rinuccio. They want to marry. Opera being the soap operas of their day (this one complete with the hypocrisy, feuding, back-stabbing and jealousy of medieval Florence), Lauretta's father has other plans for her. And so she sings to her dad the most beautiful, voluptuous, romantic aria Puccini ever composed imploring him to let them marry. Or else she'll kill herself. (Sample lyrics: 'Oh my dear papa, I love him, he is handsome, handsome . . . if my love were in vain I would go to the Ponte Vecchio and throw myself in the Arno!')

Daughters, huh.

It's thirty-two bars of concentrated teenage hormones.

The opera premiered at the Metropolitan Opera in 1918. Just over seventy years later, in 1991 in Buffalo, New York, a guy named Yvar Mikhashoff (he was actually born Ronald Mackay and, understandably affronted by such a pedestrian name, changed it to something a bit better) transcribed this aria for solo piano.

He goes nuts with it – there's even a three-handed effect in the middle of it where the melody is in the centre of the keyboard, there is a bass line underneath it and the wonderful sound of raindrops high up in the top all at the same time, so it sounds like there are two people playing it.

This is arguably the greatest tune in Italian opera (a world where there are a *lot* of great tunes) and Mikhashoff's transcription makes it even more romantic and over the top, wringing every ounce of beauty, melodrama and lust from that drop-dead-pretty melody. It is, for me, the perfect encore. I had heard Jean-Yves Thibaudet's recording of it several years previously (the only recording of it I can find) and had desperately tried to find the sheet music without success. Until, after two years of fruitless searching, a producer friend of mine asked around and came up with the goods. I'm so pleased he did – if anyone fancies a go at it then let me know and I'll send them a link to where they can buy the score. Play it for someone you love and see what happens . . .

*

VIENNA, OCTOBER 2016

I'm up at 7 a.m. in Hamburg. I've only had three hours' sleep but we need to catch a plane to get to Vienna. Despite my exhaustion I have a clear memory of the tour manager's astonished face as, forty-five seconds after my breakfast is served, I stand up and leave, having shoved a hard-boiled egg and croissant in my mouth. Simultaneously. I'm worried I won't be ready in time for the taxi and want to poo, pack and smoke, but he can't understand that. And there's no way I'm going to try and explain it to him. Especially the poo part.

I'm a mess for several reasons. None of them live-or-die reasons. But, and I don't know why, today I have no sense of perspective, all my defences are down – hence the mess.

Firstly, I freak out on the plane because I'm in row 28 which is so far at the back. I panic like crazy.

Secondly, my mind has decided to be nervous about the piano I'm going to play in Vienna. The tour schedule says it's a Bechstein not a Steinway, and it doesn't give the size, so I'm worried about that too.

Finally, I'm jittery because I've left my MacBook charger at the previous hotel. That's the second charger I've lost on this tour. Not lost. *Left behind*. Which is incredible – I don't think I've ever left anything behind in my life; I'm so goddam hyper-vigilant all the time. I'm so furious with myself. I can't decide if it's a sign I'm learning to relax and do normal things like forget chargers or if it's a sign I'm detaching from reality and losing track of things too much. And then I realise I left my toothpaste behind as well and it is Armageddon time in my head.

There's a small voice inside that is trying to acknowledge that this is not life or death. Nothing that drastic is at stake here. It's really not that important in the scheme of things. And perhaps I can breathe, take a load off my mind and just settle into this as a really nice job rather than something that always has to be utterly perfect or else life isn't worth living, just as I was telling myself after the concert in Zürich.

Maybe.

Nevertheless, it's times like this that I feel completely alone and terrified. I'm missing the rule book everyone else seems to have. So when I arrive at the hotel and ask for some tooth-paste, and they want to charge me five euros, I start crying. Because they should have it for free and I don't want to spend that amount of money even though it's nothing. But it's the principle of the thing and it feels like an injustice and a con-spiracy. I wander round Vienna looking for a shop to buy a one-euro tube of toothpaste but it's a bank holiday and literally nowhere is open. I'm hungry and tired, and have a concert in four hours. I don't feel like there is anyone in the world I can call to talk to. Because I should be better than this. I should be more mature than this, wiser, more capable. More normal. Head. Jet. Rage. Fire. Earthquake. My coping skills have done a runner, and a part of me just wants to curl up and die. From zero to suicidal in an hour.

Because it's not just that I can't touch a door handle without feeling queasy; I also can't see a good-looking guy without hating him because I assume my exes would have preferred him instead of me. I leave toothpaste in hotel bathrooms. I can't remember my computer charger. I have to pull my T-shirt over my mouth when I'm around someone who coughs.

And there I was back in London thinking that I was doing so well.

I find the only restaurant in Vienna that seems to be open and ask for a table for one. They tell me they're full. But something in my face lets the waiter know this might just about finish me off and he smiles and seats me at the bar. I order a schnitzel because it would be rude not to. Luckily, it's fucking delicious. All is not lost.

Then I wander back towards my hotel, down deserted streets, the cold air coming out of my mouth in clouds, and get safely ensconced in my room. I figure I've got two hours to sleep and I desperately need it. Emotions are exhausting. As is travel. As is always having your brain turned up to 220 degrees Celsius.

I lie there thinking, trying to relax and doing my yoga nidra, but there are intrusive thoughts breaking down the door, SWAT-style, until I have to give up. I just resign myself to the fact that this gig will be a bit shit. A nonchalant voice emerges to tell me three decent concerts out of four ain't bad.

I walk to the venue like a condemned man. I am so bored with all of it. The pressure I put on myself, the constant fear that I'm too weak and not capable of meeting my potential. All my old school reports shared the same singular refrain: James has a lot of potential but sadly isn't realising it. Perhaps back then that was because I was out of my fucking mind and broken inside. But now I'm an adult (allegedly), I am more than capable of growing up, learning, adapting and being a better version of myself.

Yet it just feels like the same old broken record keeps spinning. There is no off-switch. And no apparent hope of redemption. I am closed down. This episode is particularly bad. My tour manager can sense it – he knows I'm tolerating him as a necessary evil. The truth is, I could be finding out about his life, choosing to have dinner with him, engaging and having fun with him. But no. Head down, 'Fuck off' writ large on my face, grim determination to simply survive this next concert. There is so much I am missing out on in this world because of my head.

Like back in Bilbao, I don't over-prepare before the concert. I figure if I don't know my pieces by now then I'm fucked anyway. I'm tired and I just don't have the energy to get too worked up. I literally spend ten minutes at the piano. I try the touch, play a slow passage to figure out the sensitivity of the soft pedal and the weight of the keys, spend five minutes playing some fast passages at half speed just to get my fingers warm and supple, and then stop.

I really shouldn't have worried about the Vienna gig.

Perhaps I should have the phrase 'I really shouldn't have worried about . . .' branded into my forehead. After all that, the piano is marvellous (the schedule had said Bechstein but it's actually a Bösendorfer, a make I had heard of but I'd never played before, and boy was it special). I play well. The jigsaw pieces all fit right.

And yet. Despite the concert going well, and a mountain of piping-hot, super-delicious goulash waiting in my hotel room – something the kind house manager organised for me – I'm still back in *Reservoir Dogs* land with voices of self-doubt raging in my head.

I am convinced that it is this crushing lack of self-belief and self-esteem which is the biggest problem with me. Not just with me but, it appears increasingly likely, with society as a whole. So many of us seem to feel shit about ourselves the majority of the time and spend our lives playing catch-up to an ideal, even though we know it's false, even though we know it's unattainable, even though we know that if by some miracle we *can* attain it, it won't make a single goddam bit of difference. It's a great illusion. Like Tantalus. Just, by a hair's breadth, out of reach. My sense of worth gets topped up by a lovely audience reaction. A good review in the press. An endearing text from a girl. And that is so dangerous. Because what if those 'validations' disappear and I'm left with only my voices? What the fuck do I do when I'm all alone in serial killer land with just my head for company and it's 3 a.m?

And then it *is* actually 3 a.m., I can't fall asleep, I've meditated, used the apps, done all the things my shrink tells me to and still I'm inside my own head, raging. At anything and everything I can possibly think of. The coughing dickhead in the next-door room, the person who designed the TV in this hotel room because the power light is too fucking bright when the lights are off, the drunken Austrians walking home after a night out, the stupid idiot sheet manufacturers who used sandpaper instead of cotton, repeat on a loop ad infinitum. It feels like I've regressed so much. I can't seem to get out of this funk, just like when I was in Madrid earlier in the summer.

Eventually I take a pill. Because I can't handle another shit night of visceral self-hatred. I'm in fifty-two minds about meds even though they're no doubt appropriate for someone like me. My doc wanted me to go on something called Lyrica a few months ago, in the immediate 'parking ticket' aftermath. It's supposed to be good for anxiety and I gave it a go. But every time I took one I'd feel slightly less of a human being. I took them because I wasn't sure I'd survive the way things were going and I'd rather be medicated than dead, for now. But after a few weeks I stopped. Wanted to see if I could make it alone, as nature intended. Thus began a few weeks of off and on – a week here, a week there. Now I'm off them completely. Maybe it's pride. Maybe it's the thrill of playing my own pharmaceutical version of Russian roulette. But, other than beta blockers for performances, I don't like having to have chemical help, beyond nicotine. Which is hysterical, stupid and dangerous, because I'm not a doctor and I have no clue what's needed.

But sleep is different. My entire outlook on life, I realise on this tour, is dependent on how I sleep. After a few days of very little I'm in real danger. Which is why I get anxious. So I have Xanax with me at all times on tour. It's the only thing that works and guarantees me a full night's sleep. I limit it to once a week, twice if it's essential. Tonight's the night I take one and it's glorious. Out cold within twenty minutes, sleep until 10 a.m., no dreams, deeply relaxed, like lying in a warm bath for seven hours.

I wake up and feel like a new man. Meds like this, as long as they don't become a daily habit, are an absolute lifesaver for me.

I need to sustain this, not spiral back down to how things felt yesterday. It's my one day off, and while the emptiness stretches ahead ominously, at least it's not Concert Day with all the extra anxiety that entails. I wander round the corner where I've booked a ninety-minute massage because after all the travel and gigs, every muscle hurts. I get stretched and pounded by a masseur called Franz. It gives me the energy to cab it to an Apple Store and spend a gratuitous amount of money again on a new MacBook charger.

One ray of sunshine: I pass by a café on the way back and notice, to my astonishment, that people are smoking inside. Apparently this is still legal here. It makes my day. I sit down, order a decaf cappuccino (I've been off caffeine for nearly two years now because, well, me on caffeine makes things scary) which comes with an American amount of whipped cream on it, and I light up. I'm in heaven. The old days of smoking inside come flooding back to me. As a kid sitting in the cinema, on the top of buses, in coffee shops, at the back of airplanes . . . it feels like such a beautiful luxury.

In much better spirits I get back to my hotel and try to relax for a bit. Catch up on emails, read, watch some HBO. Perhaps today the voices of doom will leave me alone, perhaps I'll be able to enjoy my free time.

A few hours pass in this way, no meltdown, but by 5.30 p.m. I feel boxed in and claustrophobic. I need to keep moving, not thinking. I could go see the Klimt exhibition, take a long walk in the historic centre, explore the Imperial Palace, go visit any number of extraordinary sites. But that means being visible. Maybe getting lost. Touching things. Germs. Interacting. Heading out of my comfort zone. Doing something normal. Most people pay to visit cities like this; I am getting paid to do it and, as ever, all I want to do is hide. I remember how I couldn't wait to get out of the Prado museum in Madrid, after spending just a few minutes in front of Goya's *El Coloso*.

I plug in *Don Giovanni* and walk 80 metres to the same place I found yesterday which serves schnitzel. I eat alone, listening to music, staring out of the window. This particular meal takes me seven minutes to finish before I ask for the bill and bolt back to the hotel wondering why on earth I'm bothering to live like this. Because it's not really a life, is it?

Had I really made that much progress while I was in London? I'm convincing myself I really like a girl I don't even know just because she compliments me and seems kind and does fun things in bed. Then I convince myself I'll never have a 'significant other' again if I break the relationship up. I throw every ounce of energy I have at the piano while knowing I'll never be as good as I want to be or should be. I have a child the other side of the world. A career that involves me constantly making excuses for myself to myself. A tiny flat that I'm trying to dress up as something nicer than it is, with its freezer full of organic meat and soups and its £600 designer coffee table. I try and think of things coming up in my life that could ignite some spark of excitement and hope but it feels useless.

Am I the only person who looks to events in the future as a way out simply because they distract my mind from the present and allow me to kid myself that somehow, magically, it'll be different by then? It's so pathetic I shudder with revulsion.

People, kind people, good people, wise people, say to me that it doesn't have to be this way. But what if it does? You can't grow a leg back once it's been cut off. At best you get some shit prosthetic. You're still a fucking cripple with a fake appendage. It's the same being mentally ill. You can be medicated, therapised and appear to function OK. But you still believe deep down that you're a fucking asshole. Perhaps the worst thing is that I'm pretty sure I've got the tools to fix myself but I'm just choosing to decide it's too much work to control or sustain the good moments, too scary to risk choosing freedom over slavery.

Imagine telling some dude with one leg that he could actually grow another one back if he made a bit of an effort. He'd not stop until it was done. But it seems I lack the moral and spiritual backbone for that. Knowing what to do and choosing not to do it ruins any possible attempt at denial. Which only serves to increase the pathological sense of self-hatred.

I need to stop this introspection in its tracks. I can feel things unravelling. Here's where it gets dangerous quickly, especially as the evening draws in and I can feel the night calling. Clara doesn't respond to a text I'd sent three hours previously. I'm alone. I'm tired. Lonely. Under pressure. Worried about everything from money to exes to concerts to press to health and a million other things. And did I mention I am alone?

Even music isn't helping.

Because on occasion – as is happening now – music turns the volume up on the actual feelings I'm experiencing rather than changing their direction. As I sit in my hotel room, listening to Teodor Currentzis meeting Mozart's genius with his own, I spiral down into a dark cavern of self-loathing. I prefer pain to pleasure because that's what I'm familiar with. I place myself in situations that are like real-life razor blades that are going to tear me to shreds and I dive in, eyes wide open, believing that's all I'm worth. I won't care for myself unless I'm half dead and only then will I do it resentfully. I am incapable of looking at myself in the mirror without feeling such an intense level of hatred that I can't hold my own gaze for longer than a split second.

My mind has taken over. Instead of feeling just blue and a bit down and a little isolated I am, within a very few minutes, ready to leave the planet. My experience of life is suddenly like being a kid on the merry-go-round who realises he's made a terrible mistake and wants to get off. But it's too late. Everyone else is on, it's spinning round and round, a crowd of people is watching and saying 'Ah, he must be having the best time' and they mistake the look of terror on his face for one of excitement and underneath his rictus grin is pure, unadulterated terror and the realisation that the only way off this ride is to either hold on for dear life and wait until it stops, assuming that it will eventually stop, or to jump off and break your neck.

I have no idea which one to choose. I desperately want a third way. Someone to be on the horse next to me and hold my hand, something to swallow to take my mind off it for longer than a few hours, something in my ears to distract, a way to fly off the horse and float up above into the sky, and I'm looking and searching but nothing comes. This, right here, is all I've got – me, the hole, the pain.

I do the only possible healthy thing and force myself out of the hotel again and into the streets to walk. I walk and walk and don't know where I'm going. I don't recognise any street names, it's cold, I smoke and turn the volume up, amplifying everything, not just the music, walking faster and faster, trying to outrun whatever it is that wants me locked away somewhere secure.

Finally, after a couple of hours, maybe more, I stop and find a bar. I order a Coke because to drink anything stronger is to die for me and I'm not quite there yet, sit in the corner on my own, light another cigarette and start to feel the first inkling of peace. There is that place deep within me that I forget about so quickly that goes beyond all of the pain, the worry and the anxious thoughts. I find myself able to slip underneath my thoughts into that space, just for a moment, and feel a sense of letting go. I visualize my brain and just allow myself to slide into the gap behind it, leaving the noise behind.

I think of Beethoven. I'm here in Vienna, storming around the streets like an asshole and I'm desperate to feel some kind of connection with something familiar. I try and picture him 220 years previously doing the same thing. Feeling desperate, isolated, alone, withdrawn, insane. Stomping through the streets like some genius, tramp superhero. And how at odds that is with the music he wrote. I mean, yeah, of course there's anger in there, desperation, grief and all of the madness. But it's just so goddam ethereal and profound, and even when it's desperately sad it's still so beautiful. It's the opposite of what these feelings feel like – ugly, jagged, toxic, hateful. How did he manage to take those emotions and translate them into music like that? In Op. 110 specifically, how did he succeed in taking sadness, pain and hurt and turn them into wisdom, beauty and hope? And did he manage to do that in his own head? How do I find my way out of this and do the same thing?

The next morning I'm woken by angry Austrians arguing in the next-door room. I'm not sure how I got back to my room. Or when. It's 6.30 a.m. I'm travelling to Düsseldorf today for the next gig. But I figure it's, thankfully, a 6 p.m. start rather than an 8 p.m. one, remember my total lack of rehearsal and how exhausted I was for the Vienna concert, and I think, fuck it, and get up, eat breakfast and pack my bags.

I'm over halfway through this leg of the tour. I've done four gigs, with three more to go, and in a few short days I'll be back to London for a week. A week of friends, of Clara, of rest, of recharging before heading off to Barcelona, which is one of my favourite cities in the world, for a sold-out concert. It doesn't feel too unmanageable. Some of it even sounds like fun.

I know that going from wanting to die to feeling cautiously optimistic within twelve hours may seem a little weird, but it makes sense to me and seems to have become the norm. Fire on all sides; earthquake – remember? The thing that scares me more is how convincing the dark side always is. Voices telling me I want to die are infinitely more trustworthy and have a much stronger depth of feeling than the ones encouraging a sense of calm and serenity. It's the same reason I'll remember someone being an asshole to me for a lot longer than I will a beautiful sunset. Reality being dangerous, bad, hostile and dark is such an effortlessly ingrained belief that I need to really force myself to see good things as genuine, valid and sustainable.

I spend a few minutes sitting quietly in my hotel room waiting for the taxi to come to collect me. I breathe slowly and I tell myself, 'Maybe I'm wrong, maybe it is all OK, the world is safe and there is no reason not to expect good things.'

Turns out, it's not all OK. Düsseldorf is great in terms of the gig, but that night my insomnia is back with a vengeance, despite yoga, meditation, wanking, reading, downloading well-reviewed 'sleep now' apps and listening to audio books. I will not take another Xanax. I can't allow myself to make it habitual. I spent years as a teenager addicted to drugs, and falling back into that way of life is simply a form of covert suicide. If I'm going to kill myself it'll be on my terms and done my way, it won't be at the behest of big pharma even *if* my psychiatrist has prescribed them.

I don't know what to do. How do you stop something over which you have no control other than by using medication? I would give anything to be able to stop this. Anything and everything.

My mind runs away with itself, with the voices. I find myself having a massive argument with at least seven other people, all of whom only exist up there in my skull. I huddle back under the duvet at 2 a.m., close my eyes, imagine there's another human there who's warm and lying right beside me and wait for breakfast to come. I fall asleep for two hours and wake up in the middle of a nightmare. The first proper one since that spate back in September. One of the US reviews of *Instrumental* talked about the metaphorical 'haunted house' I grew up in. I still feel trapped there. Old ghosts popping up unannounced and terrifying me. In my dream, my house has been filled with wasps and hornets. Hideous, huge, terrifying ones, and they're flying everywhere, crawling in my mouth, over my face, some of them the size of pigeons.

I'm awake in bed, gasping, heart thudding. My mind is racing, all over me. I can't find a way to slow it down. If it's not the voices, it's the thousand problems, real or imagined, I think about, all of which have an additional thousand things attached to them – reactions, responses, extraneous information, implications, solutions, digressions. Someone has hacked my brain and told it to solve all of these problems along with all of their almost infinite possible permutations immediately, and not to rest until it's done it, no matter what the cost to me mentally or physically. And then they've password-protected the programme so I can't quit it. It shouldn't be this hard.

I give up on the hope of more sleep. Check my phone. There is not a single notification on the screen.

It's 4 a.m. and I've had nothing through since 10 p.m., which is unusual. I send myself an email to check my service is working. It is. As always, I'm half waiting for something magical to happen that will save me or distract me. Something will appear on my phone all of a sudden and fix all of this, at least temporarily: Clara, a business thing, a death, the lottery. I fantasise a lot about winning the lottery and I don't even play the lottery. That right there is the perfect fucking metaphor for the stupidity of my existence. I even check my spam looking for something interesting that's been placed there in error. This is how lonely I've become. The world is impossibly still and silent right now. The air doesn't move. It feels like there is no one else here on the planet with me; that sense of isolation is the curse of this fucking illness. If it is an illness. Depression? Anxiety? PTSD? Bipolar disorder? Dissociative Identity Disorder? What is it? I've been diagnosed with the lot and it doesn't help to define it. I am one person amongst seven billion. Sitting here on one planet out of eight. In one star system out of 100 billion star systems. In one galaxy out of 100 billion galaxies. I am in effect a tiny, tiny speck of dust spinning round in the middle of vast, infinite space and still my problems have no sense of perspective.

I turn on my bedside light and read a thriller on my Kindle. This one is a good one, not a McThriller. The prose is wonderful. There's a line in there about the protagonist wanting forgiveness for being damaged and allowing that damage to continue on and hurt others through his actions. I wonder if that's a cop-out or a genuine possibility. If perhaps my exes could think like that. That they could be speaking to their friends over coffee and instead of saying 'I'm just so fucking grateful I never, ever have to speak to that cunt again' they could be saying 'The guy had a pretty shitty start to life and has some really deeply held issues that aren't down to him. It's no wonder he wasn't ready for a proper relationship and wasn't that well-adjusted, but we gave it a go as best we could and honestly, I just hope he's OK. Deep down he's a good man.'

Of course they won't be saying that. I was never hosing the Dalai Lama.

I drift off again for a grand total of forty-five minutes. So, exhausted beyond belief, the next night, my second in Düsseldorf, at 9.30 p.m. I treat myself to a sleeping pill despite my determination to avoid them. I'm determined to make sure my eyes don't ping open at 4 a.m. which would make me shattered by concert time at 8 p.m. I put on some hippie sleep music complete with waterfalls and frogs and forest murmurs, and the next thing I know it's 8.30 the next morning, I've had eleven hours' sleep and I feel like I've had a three-week vacation in the Maldives. My muscles are pliable and rested, my head, after the initial deep-sleep fug has subsided, feels fresh and remarkably quiet.

You all quite want to try Xanax now, don't you?

The drive to Stuttgart is a calm four hours, the sun shining through the window. I close my eyes and drowse in the passenger seat, trying to ignore the insane autobahn speeds.

And you know what, I have this strange and very new feeling of calm surrounding my concerts now. Hitting rock bottom in Vienna has kick-started a resurfacing of sorts. Perhaps it's because I've done a few in a row in challenging circumstances that have gone well, but I hope that it's deeper than that. That there is now something resembling a kernel of self-belief about my playing that can grow and flourish, and means I can relax into concert days rather than be terrified of them and dread the fear of exposure, of messing up, of memory lapses and public humiliation. As it stands right now I have never been more chilled on the day of a concert than I am in this moment. Maybe it's got to get really bad before it gets better.

I'm not expecting it to last, but slightly alarmingly, this sense of chill doesn't go away. From the moment we arrive in Stuttgart to when I walk on stage in the most beautiful auditorium I've played in in a long time – huge chandeliers, a banquet room from a castle like some fairytale concert hall with the most perfect Steinway D sitting there under the lights just waiting for me; I feel calm.

There is still that voice that keeps saying to me, 'Ah, but if you relax now then *this* will be the one that fucks up. You're really pushing your luck now – it's been nine in a row already, it can't last. But if you think a *lot*, line things up correctly and symmetrically, wash your hands enough, flick the light switch on and off seven times at exactly the right interval, it might just be OK.' It tries to make me do my usual thing of over-re-hearsing, panicking, worrying about memory, sitting quietly running through the notes in my head, worrying about my muscles and nerves and a thousand other things. But I stop it dead in its tracks. Just like that. I actually tell it to fuck off, out loud, in the blessed privacy of my green room. Because enough already. I know I've got this. I know I can do this. And if by some chance things go wrong then there is nothing I could have done in the hour or two before the concert to prevent it. I'm sick and tired of being sick and tired and, like a toddler who knows they've finally pushed their mum to the absolute edge, with a firm talking-to, the malevolent part of my mind retreats.

Sure enough, the concert is another winner. I've never played so many gigs in a row that I am happy about. It makes no sense to me but I'm not questioning it. Somehow the approaching end of the tour fills me with reserves of energy I didn't know I had. I'm pretty sure I'll crash when I get home, but for now it's all good. I don't understand adrenalin; I only know I find it impossible to regulate. And so many concerts involving so many adrenalin spikes and crashes has to have an effect. But I haven't got properly ill, I've not felt run down other than when I haven't slept, and I'm feeling confident in my abilities.

Please, God, please can this be sustained, even if only for a little while. And not just for professional reasons – what if I can sort my work life out, feel excited and confident about my playing and relaxed around touring and press, and that then transfers to other areas of my life? What if now I am starting to get the message about work I can do the same thing with relationships, with friendships, with health and money and the anxieties around so many other areas of my life, with myself and my mind?

Then I'd have a real shot at happiness.

I've heard serenity defined as feeling peaceful and having

your feet on the ground, even when everything around you seems to be falling apart. It's easy to feel serene at the top of a mountain, chanting and doing yoga with your phone off, the closest Starbucks a thousand miles away, not a newspaper or *Daily Mail* reader in sight and nature all around you. Not so easy when you're completely out of your depth in the real world with no idea how to act around a pretty girl you quite like and an enormous amount of work pressure. But that's what I'd like to achieve. It feels like a worthy ambition. One that surely we all deserve to realise.

The next morning I'm on the train to Bonn. It's the last gig of the tour. I will have done eleven concerts in eleven cities in three weeks. It feels like a real achievement for me, for someone who has trouble getting dressed and feeding himself.

The Bonn gig is more a debate than a concert. I'm playing a few pieces but am also taking part in a discussion about both the future of classical music and the impact of music in general on the mind, in terms of health benefits and neurological implications. It's happening with a famous, rather challenging German TV personality (I'll tactfully say 'think Piers Morgan') but is actually kind of fun. Completely sold-out theatre, an engaged audience and a decent Yamaha. Denis has flown out to join me for this one too (in a moment of sadness I had called him and told him I needed a friendly face and a hug and he'd booked the tickets an hour later), which feels good. I meet some fascinating people, including a conductor I really like who wants to work with me, and a couple of neuroscientists who I secretly hope can find a fix for whatever keeps my head in overdrive.

The producers had already told me that they wanted me to play one big piece at the end, on top of a few shorter ones. This being part of the build-up to Beethoven's 250th anniversary in 2020, they asked for a Beethoven sonata. Amusingly, to me at least, on the night I ask the audience which they'd prefer – a late Beethoven piano sonata or a late Chopin piano piece. To my astonishment, and the mortification of the organisers, there is a massive vote in favour of Chopin. Which makes me chuckle.

I play them the *Polonaise-fantasie*. It goes down well. They want more, and I think, well here is possibly the most sophisticated crowd of concert-goers imaginable. I mean, Bonn + Beethoven = serious stuff, so let's try something a bit different.

So I play them Dudley Moore's amazing Beethoven parody. I tell the audience: 'I can't help feeling that if Beethoven were alive today, very, very drunk, and he was at someone's house where there was a piano, and someone said "Go on, Ludwig, improvise a tune for us", it would sound something like this.'

It opens with the theme from *The Bridge on the River Kwai* ('Colonel Bogey') and then continues in typical LVB style – all C minor, with massive chords, fugues and angst but getting weirder and weirder and more and more obviously a parody. As I play, the audience start to giggle. I start to enjoy the idea of a drunk Beethoven as the piece gets progressively more insane and ridiculous, and try as he might he just can't find a way to end it, providing several false endings in a row until, in desperation, he finally finds a way to bring it to a close (complete with a quote from the 'Moonlight' Sonata) and the entire audience are on their feet clapping and laughing. Which feels so liberating and such a lovely way to end the tour – a little reminder that this music and this industry really doesn't need to take itself quite so seriously. The presentation of classical music is so far up its own ass it could clean its teeth from the inside. And God knows Beethoven would have thought it depressing and would have desperately wanted things to change rather than have so many assholes running the shows where his music is presented. If only we could all lighten up a little and realise that music isn't some fragile, ultra-elite premium product that needs to be reserved for a certain kind of audience. That flinging open the doors and doing all we can to bring it to everyone is a far, far more noble aim than marketing high-priced seats to corporate clients and people with second homes in the Cotswolds and trust funds for their public-school educated kids.

The show ends. That's it; the tour is over. I've hit rock bottom and scrambled back out of the pit, once again. Everyone is meeting in the bar to talk and flirt and get drunk, but I just want to disappear, as ever. I make my excuses, head up to my room and order a club sandwich. I just stop everything. I eat, turn my phone off, lie on the bed and let it all wash over me. I've done it. Tomorrow I fly home and I can re-evaluate everything then.

I do allow myself to feel a little bit proud, to relax, to start to let my muscles let go a bit and the vice in my head loosen by a fraction. I've only got five days back in London before heading to Spain, but they're my five days. I can almost taste the sense of joy I'm going to get from shutting the door, unpacking, running a bath, doing the gentle, alone things I need to do.

Of course I think of Clara who is going to be waiting for me at Heathrow. I'm half expecting a text from her cancelling. I am trying hard to let go and allow whatever will happen to just happen, with her and with everything. To look at the good-ness in things instead of feeling crushed and weighed down by expectations, which in my experience are inevitably future resentments. I think perhaps I'm slowly learning to wear life a bit like a loose garment and allow things to unfold naturally, at their own pace, and without my insane, incessant, unrea-sonable demands and pathological need to control. To let go of my ideas of what's right and wrong and just be. Isn't that the best way to live?

I've no idea how long it'll last or whether this feeling of serenity and Sunday-morning chill is an echo of the post-tour comedown. But it all feels pretty good.

AFFIRMATION 7:

'I love and appreciate myself just as I am, with all my flaws and imperfections. I am good enough today and every day.'

TRANSLATION:

'I AM, JUST MAYBE, GOOD ENOUGH.'

Gluck Melody from *Orfeo ed Euridice*

The Greeks know their shit when it comes to fucked-up stories. And meze. In Gluck's opera, Euridice, the love of Orfeo's life, dies. He's heartbroken. He begs the gods to allow him to go down into the underworld and bring her back with him. They agree, subject to a few conditions, one of them being that he doesn't look back at her while they're ascending back up to life. Euridice starts to get upset as they make their way back to the real world. She thinks that he's not looking at her because he no longer loves her and pleads with him to turn and face her. Imagine a needy millennial walking stroppily behind her fella and poking him with a selfie stick, demanding he stop what he's doing and take a picture with her right now. He, powerless to refuse, complies and she is instantly killed by the gods. Harsh perhaps, but then, to be fair, anyone using a selfie stick should be annihilated immediately.

Orfeo, devastated, tries to take his own life, and everything's bleak as fuck until finally the gods take pity on their youth and beauty, bring her back to life and allow them to live and return to the real world to be together.

But before this happy ending, as Orfeo starts his uncertain journey and descends into the underworld to try to find and rescue the love of his life, there's a melody that accompanies him. It's hauntingly beautiful and perfectly encapsulates the depth of love he feels. A love that compels him, willingly, to risk death on the off chance he might get to spend a few more hours with the woman he adores. The simple, lilting accompaniment in the left hand is a near constant, giving the piece a sense of momentum, propelling him forward on his journey, while the melody sings out on top of it, a siren's call, leading him ever deeper into danger and uncertainty. But such is the power of love, such is the beauty of this music that he is content to surrender to fate and let himself go wherever life leads him. The music itself portrays this surrender; we feel him letting go, and as the music fades away into nothing, moving ever closer to the bottom register of the keyboard where it comes to a quiet, resigned, minor-key end, we, like Orfeo, just allow whatever is going to happen, happen. Happily.

*

LONDON, NOVEMBER 2016

I'm home and my body now has permission to, and does, collapse. I experience a whole new level of tiredness. Any mums reading this will snort in contempt, but I did months of night feeds when my son was born and I feel qualified to say that the fatigue I'm feeling is equivalent to having had a new child. It's so achingly boring talking about being tired. Everyone is fucking tired. The whole world needs a few extra hours' sleep each night and it's become, along with stress, the most common complaint at the water cooler, in the pub, on the internet. We're all exhausted, and even when we get eight hours we feel even worse afterwards because of the shock of it.

Things swim in front of my eyes, I can't focus, the world is detached and slow and I'm walking through treacle.

There is one thing that does get through to me despite the tiredness. For the first time in a while I've logged onto my website to answer emails from fans. I'm lucky enough to get hundreds of emails and messages from the kindest souls, every month. These people often want to share their experience, like me, of going through some of the darkness that I've written about. I read as many of them as I can when I get home and feel a deep sense of sadness. I have such a strong connection with the people who write to me, and these brave, powerful messages are so overwhelming. I find myself once again just desperately sad at the level of pain that makes up such a big part of our world.

I need a cushion sometimes. A buffer from the reality of life and its attendant pain. Something or someone to protect me and dilute things. Which is why it's so hard to be alone and so tempting to want to spend time with the Claras of this world. She had met me at the airport. With flowers and everything. I had brushed my teeth on the airplane specially. We have dinner and she stays the night. I can't sleep and am up and about from 5.30 a.m., having given up hope of finding even an hour of rest. But it just doesn't bother me, for once. I spend an hour or two just lying there in bed enjoying the feeling of a real warm human being slumbering beside me, which is so nice after having imagined it all these nights during the tour. My head is remarkably still. My thoughts slower than usual and less frequent.

After she's gone I do my piano practice, have a walk and clean the car. I still feel drunk with tiredness, but it's actually not unpleasant. I wonder if I could perform while feeling like this, whether it would affect my coordination and muscle strength too much. I indulge in imagining I could do it – the bliss of knowing I don't actually need rest, that adrenalin, my dear friend Dr Theatre, will always take care of it for me even with no sleep, that I can relax and let go. Ironically, if I really believed this I would no doubt sleep like a baby. But perhaps I am just wired up to worry. It's a self-fulfilling vicious circle that all insomniacs know inside out – don't sleep, feel exhausted, get anxious I won't sleep again the next night, that anxiety keeps me awake, don't sleep et cetera et fucking cetera.

I wonder if all self-help gurus or people who have achieved enlightenment are actually just completely worn out and therefore incapable of summoning up the energy to get riled up. Is there a correlation between spiritual growth and insomnia? Perhaps that's the secret to serenity. Or maybe I've just had enough shit kicked out of me to stop caring so much. There's a big gap between not sweating the small stuff and simply not giving a fuck about anything or anyone, and I worry I'm doing the latter right now.

Like Clara. It's wonderful having her around, but I'm realising by this stage that we're quite different, and I'm definitely just using her to fill a hole. Clara could be anyone really; haven't we all at some point had that gut-wrenching sense of aloneness and desperate need to be close to someone, an urge to grab and hold on to the first person that shows us even the slightest kindness? I know what's coming, and I know it's not fair on her.

I'd always feared I'd turn into this cynical, nasty, quite spiteful person eventually. That life would somehow find a way to corrode that part of me that's better than its shadow, that's good and decent. I'd end up like the angry men living alone with rancid dishes piled high in their sinks, fridges empty save for suspect cheeses and remorseful beers, frayed jumpers pulled tight over pot bellies and shaving foam behind their ears, morning drinkers blaming their ex-wife of thirty years ago for their current problems.

It's becoming more and more tempting to head down that route. I would become closed down. Surly and uncommunicative. If people bored me I'd simply tell them they bored me rather than smile, nod and ask appropriate questions. I'd live a quiet life, with the occasional lightning flash of lonely anger. I don't want it to happen but sometimes it feels like the easiest way out of all this. Ideally I could find some kind of middle ground – being too tired to care about the stupid things but without turning into a callous, bitter asshole. That's what I want. To live a life where the few really important things are valued and cared about and the trivial things aren't given so much power and weight.

I look at my diary and speak with Denis to figure out what the next few weeks are looking like: trips and gigs in Spain and the UK, a three-day recording session, plus press and talks and other work stuff. I find myself speaking about it in a tone that is weary and slightly dejected. And yet I could so easily insert so many exclamation marks in my conversations with him – trips to Spain! A recording session! Things I've wanted my whole entire life are happening and unfolding, and I'm treating them like a chore once more.

Maybe I'm still feeling a bit bruised about Vienna, and I have a fear of going back to that state of mind.

I stop myself then and there. There's a fork in the road. This, right now, is the time to be enjoying the things I've worked so hard for, and these are the stories that one day, perhaps, I'll be telling my grandchildren when they've been bribed enough to come and visit the scary, smelly man in hospital. Surely this time is worth celebrating? I take a few minutes to sit and really look at what's happening in my life right now. To acknowledge the amount of good and the sense of adventure in it. I think, and, surprisingly, so do a few of the head-gang, that it's time to start enjoying life rather than enduring it.

I'm closer than ever to having all the tools I need to make that happen, to being grateful for the life I have. The life I really want is achievable, I'm sure of it. I can even see just how the perfect fantasy day would play out.

It would look something like the following, if I ever manage to nail it.

Warning: this passage reads suspiciously like something all the gurus and self-help books promise you you'll achieve *if* you follow their instructions to the letter. You won't. It's just not possible. But, as an (academic) insight into what one could come close to achieving with a lot of work, it's something to aspire to, I think. So here's my version of Lou Reed's 'Perfect Day'.

Fantasy Day

I wake up at 8.45 a.m. I've been awarded a lie-in today. No idea why. But I open my eyes and something unusual is happening. It's quiet. I mean it's quiet inside my head as well as outside. I feel rested. I realise it's Concert Day and I feel, well, calm and a little bit excited.

The actual fuck?

I get out of bed and poke my head around the door to the living room, half expecting an ambush. Nothing. Beautiful sunlight streaming in, stillness, peace.

I make a cup of tea and stand at the window staring out at the world. Things feel manageable. I got eight hours' sleep and feel invincible as a result. This is what it must feel like to wake up slowly and gently like I've seen in movies and read about in books. I let my body ease itself awake, allow my mind to gently catch up with itself while I drink tea and put some porridge on the boil.

Fragments of piano pieces come into my head and I find myself so excited about playing them live tonight. I've got some pals coming down to watch and can't wait to see them and maybe grab a burger afterwards. Denis won't be there, but that's fine. I know what I'm doing and can easily deal with the shit he usually has to deal with on the night of a gig.

I feel so much lighter than usual, but my arms feel strong. Not muscular strong. Piano strong. Secure and confident in what they're going to be doing later. Ready to perform, to push themselves, to do something remarkable and blast out fifty thousand notes into the ether. Normally I'd head to the piano now, slightly panicky, and rehearse, but I take my time with breakfast and then think, fuck it, I want to go for a walk. So I head outside, hook a left onto Elgin Avenue and walk the half mile up to Starbucks, careful to use a maximum of two adjectives to describe the coffee I want (tall and decaf).

It's not yet 10 a.m. but the sun is shining and I sit outside and light up my first cigarette of the day. I forgot to bring my phone. I smile at people walking past me on their way to wherever it is they're going. I feel so goddam lucky to be heading into town later to play the piano for people and get paid for it.

It occurs to me that acceptance and openness is the magic. My heart is usually closed. I tend to scowl at people, judge them constantly – too fat, too thin, ugly, rich, poor, stupid, slow, badly dressed, handsome. But today it's open and there's light blazing out of it. It's as if during the night I've released decades' worth of crusty, held-on shit that is way past its sell-by date. We live in a world of feelings created only by our thoughts. The actual reality of my situation is simply factual and has zero impact on my mood and feelings, but my *thoughts* about that reality can turn a perfect day into a suicide note. I ask myself, what if my thoughts were just a bunch of clouds, hot/cold air with no substance? And me, I'm the sky, infinite and with endless possibilities. The clouds can just drift through, passing by in their own time, but the sky is always there and safe and vast, and that's where I can choose to spend my time, inhabiting that place of refuge. What if doing what it took to feel peaceful and content was more important than chasing the dubious and temporary approval of others?

Cigarette goes in the ashtray on the table, not the gutter,

and I stroll home in the sunshine, really ready now to rehearse, warm up, explore the constant new surprises that I find in Beethoven and Chopin.

There's no rushing. No mania. No static in my brain. I'm just present and focused. Mindfulness in action. It feels amazing. I glide onto my piano stool and start to work. Slowly, methodically. It all feels solid and secure: the notes, the memory, the tone, the touch. After an hour and a half I know that I'm good to go. And it's not even 12.30 yet.

I call Matthew and arrange to meet for a coffee and a stroll through the park. I don't need to be at the venue until 4 p.m. and it's a beautiful day. I walk the four thousand steps into Marylebone, but as it's Currentzis playing Mozart I'm listening to I kind of float there. I meet my best friend and my goddaughter and we walk through Regent's Park. I notice the trees, the colours, listen attentively to what my friend is saying, feeling alert and calm.

We sit in the café eating something delicious while chatting. I've not looked at my phone, which I brought with me this time, more as an afterthought, once. It occurs to me that perhaps the most beautiful thing in the world we can do is to truly listen to someone else.

I occasionally remember I'm going to perform this evening and it makes me smile. I've got my stage clothes in a bag with me. Along with a protein bar and a book. After Matthew and his beautiful little girl disappear, I sit for a while reading. My son calls me just before he goes to band practice and we have a laugh over the phone.

I get to the venue dead on 4 p.m. Not an hour early like

usual. The crew are all there to meet me and we set up the lights quickly and efficiently. I try the piano, spending ten minutes warming my fingers up and getting used to the sound and touch. It all feels good. Microphone is checked and everything is locked down and set for the evening's show.

By 5 p.m. I'm backstage, reading quietly again. I'm snacking on my protein bar and a banana and occasionally responding to Denis who is checking in on me. I let him know everything is fine.

I turn my phone off an hour before the show starts. I listen to the humming from the speaker as the hall fills up and am grateful there are so many people attending.

I start to feel the thrill of adrenalin and butterflies, but they're welcome feelings. Third-date feelings when you've met her before and know she's beautiful, kind and gentle. And a little bit filthy.

One minute before the start, I'm waiting in the wings, stage manager next to me, audience settling down, fingers and hands warm and tingling, muscles calm, mind quiet, looking forward to doing this. Looking forward to it!

I perform well. I don't lose my focus. I let myself off the hook when the occasional passage goes awry. It went awry because I was taking a risk and trying something new. Sometimes it works, sometimes it doesn't. It's always worth doing regardless.

I appreciate the audience. Even make eye contact with one or two of them as I speak. I don't see them as hostile or indifferent or bored. I see them as friends, many of whom I just haven't met yet. I play for all of them while constantly marvelling at what

Beethoven managed to achieve with his phenomenal mind. I lose time in a safe way, lose myself in a safe way, and by the end of the concert I'm exhausted, spent but happy.

I text Denis to let him know that it went well and head off to the signing where I meet people, maintain eye contact, remember names, dedicate books and CDs and appreciate every moment because these guys have not only bought tickets but have also shelled out for a book or an album as well.

I wait until everyone's done, thank the crew and jump in a cab home. I walk through the door to an empty but warm flat. It's peaceful and nicely lit. It feels like someone's home rather than an empty shell. I turn the heating on and make a cup of tea. I spend a few minutes updating and checking Twitter and returning some emails.

I wander into the kitchen and pan-fry a tuna steak for a couple of minutes each side, just like it says on the Jamie Oliver website. I slice some beetroot, avocado and mozzarella and chuck in some leaves to make a salad to accompany it. Toast some bread. Made with linseed stuff that apparently is good for you.

I eat at my dining table. The TV is off. There is no noise. I'm just there, eating, alone with my thoughts and feeling comfortable with the day and hopeful about tomorrow, whatever it may bring. I run through the concert, looking at what worked and what could be improved. Make a few notes and mark some scores in places where I want to tighten up memory or work on the fingerwork. After I finish eating I set them on the piano ready for practice tomorrow, clear up, make sure the kitchen is tidy and treat myself to a couple of episodes of *Curb*

Your Enthusiasm before jumping in the shower and then into bed. Clean sheets. Warm room. Comfortable. Smelling nice. Peaceful. Quiet.

I grab my notebook and write down ten things I'm grateful for and ten things I've done for other people that day. I read a couple of chapters from a new book from one of my favourite authors (spy fiction, brilliantly written, scary, thrilling, intelligent – do read Charles Cumming and Henry Porter, you won't regret it) and then turn out the light.

I do my yoga nidra lying down, working my way through my entire body. After about fifteen minutes I start to drift off, slowly and gently. My thoughts are sleepy and kind and soothing. The adrenalin levels have tapered off nicely and there's this restful, supportive voice in my mind lulling me into sleep. It tells me I've had a good day. I've done well. I can be proud of myself. It thinks gently about people close to me – my son, my friends, my support network – and doesn't sound suspicious, angry, paranoid, resentful or on alert. I'm aware of how many people I've got in my life who are willing to walk however far it takes to help me out. And that I can and do reciprocate.

As I sleep I dream weird, wonderful, interesting dreams.

That's the goal for me, although seriously, who lives like that? But there are elements within it that are not completely fantastical and that are largely doable, while allowing for a certain amount of normal life to throw the odd curveball your way. Like an occasional inability to sleep, for example.

During that week before I leave for Spain, I have the biggest attack of insomnia I have ever endured.

Ironic, isn't it? Just as things were getting better. Not fantasy-self-help-bullshit better, just a bit better. It's as if my mind and body can't take too much of what is 'normal' and good, and has to go back to its habitual self-destructive ways if I dare start to enjoy things a bit too much.

I don't sleep longer than an hour or two at a stretch every night. When I do sleep it's filled with nightmares – terrible dreams again about childhood, fatherhood, the future, the past. My subconscious is doing the best it can to process the things I need to deal with against my wishes, and there's no doubt it's going to find a way to come out eventually. Probably some kind of cancer or (another) psychotic break. But if I can just hold that off a bit longer, a few more years, until my career is a bit further down the line, I've got enough cash to cover the medical bills, set my son up in a decent flat, lived a little bit longer, experienced a few more good things, travelled to a few more places, I'd be really grateful.

I am so desperate to sleep that I try everything – except the pills, I have to resist the pills. When I was in hospital they medicated me the entire time I was there, 24/7, and those memories are still so awful that taking sleeping pills brings back those feelings of powerlessness, hopelessness and despair with a vengeance. I also know that if I start taking them regularly I will not only get addicted to them but my tolerance will increase and I'll need to take higher and higher dosages in order for them to work. It's a cycle I have to avoid. I try to find other solutions. I visit an acupuncturist, get needles thrown strategically into my feet (it helps the adrenal glands, apparently), head, hands and back. No difference.

I hit the local homeopathy store, despite knowing it's the biggest crock of shit there is. Me, who holds homeopathy in the same contemptuous category as tarot cards and psychics. I explain to the herbal-smelling hippie behind the counter that I need to sleep, desperation in my voice, and could he recommend anything at all. He tells me they have lots of suggestions and I ask for his most effective one.

'Ah, that's impossible to say as they effect people differently,' he answers kind of smugly, the 'obviously' implicit in his tone.

'I can recommend this one, however.'

He puts a vial of pills on the countertop.

'It has valerian in it and can be quite powerful. You only need to take one. Are you OK with sugar pills or would you prefer a different kind of base?'

'I fucking love sugar. That's not a problem.'

He looks at me funny.

'OK. Have you also considered cupping?'

'Cupping what?'

'No, "cupping" – using hot cups to promote blood flow on your back. It can be very helpful, especially for you, as I think you're quite Vata.'

<Astonished stare>

'Perhaps Vata-Kapha. It's Ayurveda.'

<Hatey eyes>

'There's also this spray that works well. Three sprays under the tongue before bed.'

He hands me a tube.

I look at it. Turn to him. 'This says it's suitable for use on babies.'

'Oh, yes. It's very supportive for little ones. For the whole family in fact.'

He seems proud.

This is when I lose it.

'You want to give me something you use on babies. To make me sleep. I weigh at least ten times more than a baby. Even a really fat baby. I'm forty-one years older than a baby. I've built up a tolerance to so many drugs that Valium, Seroquel, Ambien, Clonazepam and Zopiclone won't even touch me any more. And you think three sprays of *baby juice* is going to send me off to sleep?'

'Well, perhaps if you smudge your bedroom first with sage wood and – '

I leave the store.

Return and grab the pills he had recommended earlier, shoving a tenner on the table.

You never know, right?

He has told me to take one (they're powerful, remember) so I take two, and nothing. Not a goddam thing. Then I take another two. Still nothing. I imagine him smirking as I left the shop. I'm just another fucking mug.

At my wits' end, I go the next day for something called a sound bath. I lie down on the floor of a warm, dark, comfy flat in Maida Vale while a young guy puts pillows under my head and a blindfold on me and then plays an assortment of instruments (mainly gongs and singing bowls) for an hour. It's quite a trip, and even though I'm wriggly and wired from

no sleep for nearly a week now, it does calm me down. For
fifteen minutes.

I still don't sleep.

I get a massage from an ex-bodyguard, karate-fighting, rug-
by-physio, brick-shithouse Algerian called Farouk that almost
leaves me hospitalised. It is unbelievably painful. Fingers digging
into muscles that have no business being poked and prodded. I
can't walk for two days afterwards and still don't sleep.

I cancel everything. Film premiere at the Albert Hall, dinner
with friends, dates with Clara, meetings with publishers. I
just have this overwhelming urge to batten down the hatches
and hide out, undisturbed and alone. I don't trust myself to
be around people and I don't trust what might come out of
my mouth. Because, of course, as you and I know by now, if I
don't sleep, it becomes dangerous. Everything is so much more
acute when it's like this, all my quirks are amplified tenfold.
This time I cannot step on pavement cracks, not because of a
sense of discomfort, but because of a feeling of genuine terror.
I squeak and grunt and tic and twitch much more than usual.
I repeat words and phrases, tap specific rhythms out with my
fingers, flick switches, position and reposition items on tables.
I try to do crosswords to keep my mind vaguely sharp but I
can't get the letters to fit just right in the little boxes and have
to stop, ripping the paper up and sobbing. It's all so goddam
exhausting. Sending texts takes me for ever because I have to
tap the screen on my phone in a specific way, forced to hit the
wrong letters because that particular part of the screen *has* to
be touched and if it's not done exactly right I have to delete it
all and start again. Phones are thrown at the wall in frustration,

nothing feels safe to touch, I spend too much time sitting alone, terrified to do anything other than stare into space.

By the middle of the week the voices in my head have been full-on raging at me, squadron-commander style, for days. There's a constant stream of invective hurled my way. The left side of my face is twitching and spasming all the time. My adrenal glands feel shot, I can't focus, I don't know what to do, I manage not to engage with the voices but I can't silence them either. I'm stuck in a repetitive loop of self-hatred and punishment and can't find any way to break the cycle and get out. A rat in a maze but minus the scientists and the rewards.

I call Matthew and cry down the phone to him (not quite like the Regent's Park walk admiring the leaves and the squirrels that was in my fantasy). He comes over – he always comes over – and we have dinner and talk for ages. It's helpful.

I stay off Twitter as much as possible, don't read the newspapers, avoid my phone as best I can and only leave the house to walk. I wander aimlessly, without music and headphones this time (the choice of what to listen to is too overwhelming), and look peculiar because there are a lot of cracks to hobble over and I don't want the world to end. I'm in a right state.

I feel like I did when I was walking to the school gym all those years ago. Terrified, knowing that what was coming was inevitable and nothing could change it but still, against all the odds, hoping and waiting desperately for something or someone to stop things, for some giant magic hand to descend from the sky and whisk me away to safety knowing all the time that there would be no such luck. There is a palpable sense of powerlessness in that specific flavour of 'child who can see something utterly awful about to happen to them and has to voluntarily walk towards it and endure it regardless'. It makes me want to weep in frustration and panic, and reach up through my nostrils and pull my brain out, flicking chunks of it into the street until it's all gone and I can finally experience some fucking peace and quiet. I don't make eye contact with anyone. I stop for coffees and sit and smoke and try and make sense of things that are nonsensical. I draw a blank.

I see my shrink. She's concerned and suggests yoga and exercise. Both of which I do. Neither of which work.

I end things with Clara. I've not got the resources to carry on. And better to do it now than fuck her up for the next few months. I try and be firm but kind, but it's doubtless dismissive and cruel. It's necessary though, and the truth is that even if I *was* healthy enough I wouldn't want a relationship with her. She tells me she feels she can help support me and share her resources until I have enough of my own, but I don't buy it. Even if that were possible, I'd be in her debt, and past experience tells me that it's only going to be future ammunition for her to use against me. The very idea of interacting with someone on an intimate basis right now is incomprehensible to me. I wish I could find a way to explain that to her that doesn't sound selfish. The problem is that it *is* selfish. My mind is that over-tired toddler who has simply decided he has had enough and starts to melt down in the middle of the supermarket. There is not a thing that anyone can do to stop it. I can barely look after myself; how the fuck can I expect to act decently and kindly with another human being?

So I take the easy option and run. I would rather be single for ever than add 'taking into account another person's feelings' to my list of things to do at the moment. I'm running on vapours and need to do everything and anything necessary to conserve fuel. I feel like I'm experiencing that thing where someone has hypothermia and their body automatically starts to shut down bit by bit to divert resources and keep the brain alive. I am furiously chucking appendages and organs out of the window in a desperate attempt to preserve what's left of my mind.

I play some piano, check my memory of the pieces I'm playing. My muscles feel weak and don't do what I want them to. My hands aren't working properly. I see them playing the notes but they seem to belong to someone else. I'm not able to focus. My memory is full of holes. I'm scared.

I get the distinct impression that this mental state has now reached the point of no return. That I'm down the rabbit hole again, and rather than turn back and find my way out, I need to find a way through this by going forward, not backwards.

I figure I need to sustain myself for three more weeks in order to get through the series of concerts I'm going to be giving in Spain, a talk in London and gigs in Bristol and Cheltenham. I am recording the new album near the end of December, just before my son comes over for Christmas. Then I can take two whole weeks for myself to fall apart quietly and safely. Maybe in a warm, safe hospital. I'm pretty sure my psych ward loyalty card is still active.

This time-mapping brings some measure of comfort. It makes the next three weeks seem bite-sized and manageable. I know it's an illusion, that in December there'll be something else I'm worried about and I will undoubtedly just need to get to

January, when I'll just need to get to March and on and on. But it gives me enough of a lift to not feel so completely desperate. It allows me enough peace of mind to feel that perhaps this is doable, and that even though I'm now seeing double and can barely function, the adrenalin will kick in when I'm due to perform, my muscles will work fine and I'm not going to lose the rest of my sanity along with my livelihood. I'm now in the last stretch of the marathon, finish line and foil blankets in sight.

I print out a calendar for those three weeks and once again remove anything that isn't completely essential. I turn down an offer to support a friend of mine on stage at Brixton Academy even though it could be fun. It's just too much right now and I'm scared that a noisy rock audience trying to make sense of Rachmaninov being pelted at them across a huge PA may not go down too well, despite his assurance they'd love it and he would too.

I finish off by making lists. That old chestnut. Something that my control-freak head just loves. Lists are good for me, reassuring, comforting, relaxing. Lists of everything: food I need to buy; pieces I'm currently performing; pieces I'm soon recording; pieces I'm going to be performing next year; things I need to pack for concerts abroad; days until I can rest; days off between now and the end of the year; how much money I have currently; how much is coming in over the next few months; things to buy for the flat; countries I'm going to visit next year; movies and TV shows I want to watch; albums I want to buy; ditto books etc. etc.

As I do this, my mind quietens down somewhat and I realise that perhaps I, we, all have a limited number of fucks to give away. And that I have been far, far, far too generous in giving them away. I give a fuck about Sky not having the latest episode of *Criminal Minds* to download. Being told I can't use the business-class loo on an airplane and need to walk to the back of the plane to piss. I don't have the correct change for parking. A restaurant doesn't have a table for me. My phone battery life isn't long enough. There's a dude taking too long to pay in a shop when I'm waiting anxiously behind him. A thousand and one things that are of no importance whatsoever. But to me they're all big, giant, massive problems that I have to solve, blame people for, argue in my head about. It's been decades of working on myself and nothing has changed. I still sweat the small stuff. And by sweat I mean shit my pants and want to kill people.

I think if as a kid you face some really, really serious problems that you cannot solve and no one around you seems able or willing to solve them for you, then the big fear is that it will always be like that, even as an adult, and all of your problems will for evermore seem unsolvable. So if I can deal with the little ones then at least it's a start. I can maintain the illusion that I am at least a little bit powerful and able to control certain outcomes. Even if that means just being able to get a takeaway coffee within a certain self-defined time frame.

It's such bullshit. And it's doubly painful because I realise I'm doing it, then get pissed at myself, and that just increases the amount of fucks given and I get even more angry, and round and round we go.

When I was twenty-eight and hadn't played the piano in a decade, I left a high-paying, secure job in the City to pursue a ridiculous childhood dream of becoming a concert pianist. I made it too. I really went and did it. I've got the albums and concerts and reviews to prove it. And, despite being told I was a bit shit and not very smart in school, I wrote a book. A couple of books. I can pay my bills and earn a decent living doing what I love and what the whole world kind of snorted at in contempt when I told them it was what I was going to do.

I managed to do this because I really gave a fuck about that. Because it was worth it. Just like I give a fuck about my son. My friends. Music. My health (sometimes). And doing the right thing. Pretty much everything else, I'm wasting my supply on. It needs to stop. Not in an aggressive way. Just in a 'this isn't working for me any more so I'm going to start letting certain things go' way. Like when someone doesn't text me back within a time frame I deem acceptable – I'll wait. Or lawyers doing what they're being paid to do – I'll accept that. Or Sky not having the right fucking TV show – I'll watch a DVD. That passive-aggressive hotel minibar where they fleece you £7 for a bottle of water? You know what, fuck you, I'm good with the tap. Also, it has fluoride in it.

There must be millions of people out there who have figured out how to get through a day without wanting to die or kill. It *must* be possible. I am not the only one struggling with these thoughts, no matter how bad they get, and I'm convinced that others have felt and do feel and will continue to feel the same way. I am not alone and in solitary confinement even if it feels like it.

After I've written my lists, I go to bed. I feel slightly calmer. And, without any meds, I sleep straight through for seven hours for the first time in for ever. There are no unpleasant dreams, no night sweats, no 4 a.m. terrors. Just rest, regeneration and restoration. Everything sleep should be. I wake up feeling confused but soft and slightly shocked. I wonder if it will last, if I can pin down the exact sequence of events, routines and rituals that have made this possible, and hope desperately that it isn't a one-off.

Miracle of miracles, the next night it happens again. I sleep without chemicals, my body pathetically grateful for being allowed to do what it has so needed to do and used to be able to do naturally and effortlessly, albeit a long, long time ago.

I get to the end of another gentle, productive day of piano and walking and cups of tea with a friend and sink into bed realising that I am almost living in my Fantasy Day. It feels amazing.

And then it's Monday morning. I pack my bag, empty the fridge of perishables, charge up my aggressively long list of devices (Kindle, hi-res music player, external battery packs, laptop, phone, iPad, toothbrush and more), all the while thinking, how did travelling get this dependent on plug sockets (my toothbrush has its own iPhone app, for God's sake), put the house to sleep for a week and hop on the tube to Victoria where I grab the Gatwick Express and head to the North Terminal for the two-hour flight back to Spain.

SPAIN, NOVEMBER 2016

After a day in Valencia doing a press conference, I am heading back to Barcelona by train.

Spanish trains fucking rock. There's just no two ways about it. They go at 300kph, I got served a four-course meal (having paid under seventy euros for a ticket), they're clean, leave and arrive dead on time and put the Swiss/Germans to shame. Christ, my train was playing *High Fidelity* on TV screens in every carriage (free headphones available on demand)! It doesn't get cooler than that. They also make us in Britain look like a total fucking embarrassment when it comes to public transport. But then we all know that anyway, don't we? Spain may be broke, but at least they have something to show for it.

There's a mum on the train with her two-year-old son who's crying at the table next to me. She gets out her phone and starts playing him a video of 'Stairway to Heaven' (I shit you not). Jimmy Page calms the kid down and he stares, transfixed and listening. I want to give her a Mother of the Year award.

Music really does do it all.

Barcelona is such an awesome fucking city – welcoming, alive, vibrant, relaxed. I'm hoping that five or six days here will seep into my head and work its magic. It's cold but bright and I'm driven to the hotel by one of the organisers of an international jazz festival. It's the first time they've ever had classical music performed as part of the festival, which makes me happy. Keith Jarrett recorded Mozart piano concertos, Oscar Peterson was classically trained and adored it, Ravel used to hang with Gershwin in Harlem jazz clubs, chain-smoking and talking shit together over whiskey. And Nina Simone said that it was Bach who made her dedicate her life to music. So it belongs here as much as anything else. The icing on the cake is that mine is the first and quickest concert to sell out. I'm thrilled because it's another one in the bank for Chopin and Beethoven, and tops up my self-esteem a few notches.

The hotel is awesome. New, boutique but not in a hipster way, and my room has a private courtyard with rocking chairs where I can sit in the sun, smoke and drink coffee. It couldn't be more perfect. Except that the next day, I start to feel properly sick. I've been fighting off this cold and, as is so often the way, my body knows I can't get sick because I simply have to be fit to perform. But the German tour has taken its toll and I'm feeling pretty lousy on this day which is filled with interviews. It's compounded tenfold by the announcement that Donald Trump has become the leader of the free world. The news leaves me, and everyone else, reeling. The world is spinning off its axis and we're all guilty of the bystander effect. It feels even more of a shock than Brexit, which was a shameful enough act for at least one generation. It seems it's not just me, but rather there is a collective desire to self-implode.

Every single interview that day begins with 'What do you think of Trump becoming president?' I have an urge to say to them that I'm not a gynaecologist but I definitely know a cunt when I see one. But there really aren't any words to describe how I feel, so I just tell them it's terrifying, sickening and a fucking outrage, and God help us all. And we move on to talking about music and more gentle subjects, like *How to Play the Piano*, which is just out in Spain with the most exquisite jacket. Got to keep plugging merchandise to make the publishers happy . . .

Concert Day arrives and I'm properly achy, fluey and miserable. I can't fend it off any longer.

I've got a morning interview with a big radio station, which

I'm dreading, because I'd much rather stay in bed, and because journalists give me the heebie-jeebies.

A few years ago I got a bunch of Facebook and text messages from people I hadn't spoken to in twenty years saying someone from the *Mail on Sunday* had called them asking about me, what I was like as a kid, did I do drugs, any particular memories stand out and so on. Worst of all, the guy said, 'Oh yeah, James knows I'm calling you, we're doing a story on him – he's fully aware of it.' Fucking asshole. This was the first I'd heard of it. Lawyers did their thing, nothing was printed; I don't even know what they were looking for (or found), or whether it was just fishing. All of which goes to say, if you read anything in the *Mail on Sunday* in which sources close to me from years ago verified that I had a penchant for clown porn as a teenager, it's not (completely) true.

It made me a little wary of the press. Which I hate, because I want to talk about things openly, it's so important to be open and talk about our pasts, and feeling like it's not safe to do so isn't helpful.

One guy from the *Sunday Times* seemed to ambush me a few months ago and kept asking me questions about a topic I really didn't want to talk about at all (*so* not telling you what). But he wouldn't let it go. And eventually I asked him if we could go off the record. He agreed and I told him why I didn't want to talk about that particular issue. To his credit he honoured it. But he then called Denis and told him to tell me that 'off the record' simply doesn't exist any more. He'd honour it because he was old school, but that I must never, ever, under any circumstances, *ever* ask to go off the record again with a journalist because they'd nod and say 'sure thing' and then print whatever the fuck they wanted. He told me that when being interviewed at home I should be extra careful – journalists will ask to use the bathroom and go through your cabinets, while leaving the recording device still rolling on the table in the hope it will catch something juicy while they're out of the room.

So yeah, I'm a bit wary of journalists.

I finish up the radio interview (which, as it turns out, was refreshingly lovely) and go for a long walk around Barcelona. I have a profound urge to move here (or Madrid – both cities are an embarrassment of loveliness and I just can't decide which one to choose). I'd rent a little apartment, spend a year or two here, learn Spanish, eat well, soak up the relaxed atmosphere, give concerts, write, adopt the siesta habit with the deep gratitude of a very tired person and hunker down in one of the most beautiful cities I've ever had the honour of visiting. There is nothing stopping me – no ties to London any more; my son can easily come and stay with me in Catalonia or Madrid whenever he wants, I'm two hours away from London if I need to be there for anything. I draft an email to Jan, my Spanish publisher, asking him to recommend a few estate agents for me in each city. I don't send it yet. But I have a plan brewing. Get through to early next year where I'm away for most of the first three months in South America and New York and then get the fuck outta Dodge and move to Spain. Just in time for a proper summer.

I'm so unwell that after my walk all I can do is crawl into bed at 2 p.m., foregoing practising. I have an afternoon nap, which does the trick, because it's one of the best concerts I've ever given – one where everything just comes together. I've a couple of friends who have flown out from London for it and I feel proud and happy they've been here for this. The queue for signings is ridiculous but filled with such generous people that I forget how hungry I am and sit there just enjoying saying hey and listening. At around 11.45 p.m. I'm all done and a bunch of us – my mates, Denis, the promoters, and Jan – head to a restaurant for dinner. Yep. Midnight dinner in Barcelona. This feels exactly how it should feel after a gig. Not terrified, chastened and ashamed, heading back to a solitary hotel room by myself, but out celebrating, enjoying the moment.

I make a mental note to remember the link between not practising the piano that day, a carefree walk around the city and a lovely long afternoon nap and what was, for me, such a good performance. Concerts are so much a mind game. Well, everything is really, isn't it? Dating, working, sport, sleeping, living ... Diffusing the self-imposed pressure, being relaxed, positive, confident and less anxious leads to a much better performance on and off the stage. I think perhaps I'm finally figuring out how to do this wonderful job of mine while enjoying it. Evidently I'm going to have to have more than a few painful, false starts before it starts to stick, but more and more often over the past few weeks I'm starting to feel like I'm getting there.

I'm up until 3 a.m. but don't even care. I've made sure the next day is completely clear and just for me. I sleep in, wake up lazily, still feeling good about myself. My friends and I decide to jump on a train to Figueres, an hour outside of Barcelona, and go visit the Dalí museum. Because I never do things like that and

I'm starting to understand that my life is only going to improve by doing the things that go against what my head instructs me to do. Like getting on a train and going to a museum rather than being alone in my hotel room for eight hours.

We have a wonderful time looking at the messed up mind of Dalí laid bare, without apology, for us all to witness. So different to my visit to the Prado. We end up back in Barcelona late in the evening at a restaurant called Flax & Kale (my friends are veggie) and it's surprisingly good, even for a committed meat-eater like me. Evidently there is a closet hipster inside me, waiting to get out – who knew grilled watermelon and goat's cheese would be such a winning combination?

This snapshot of my life right now is so perfect. If I were watching it on a TV screen I'd be so happy for myself. I've worked hard for this. I've had a great few days in Spain and I need to think about how to continue like this. Because as ever there is the nagging voice from deep down still growling at me that it's not real, it's not sustainable. It can't last. Shouldn't last. I don't deserve this.

Fire on all sides; earthquake. I'm scared that that part of me that wants to live and live well is too weak to compete with the deep-down voices who tell me it can't last and that, realistically, I'm only biding my time pretending to function until I'm out of here.

Things don't fall apart when I'm back in London, but what I do do is, once again, cancel everything in my diary for the next four days – except for a record label meeting because I'm not brave enough to let business take a back seat, even for a few days – and come up with a plan, based on that last week of joy in Spain. I'm so close to something amazing now, I want to give it some time, and focus on getting it really right. I don't know how many more false starts I can endure. I am determined to pull my mental socks up and try harder to be happier and find a little more freedom in my picture-pretty perfect life. To stop thinking quite so much and start just being, enjoying life moment to moment. That old-school *Times* journalist had called me a 'complicated man' in his interview, and he wasn't just being tactful, he was bang on. My mind is an indecipherable IKEA manual, and all this time, rather than simply using some common sense and intuition, I've been trying in vain to follow the instructions. I want to burn those instructions and start again.

Whatever it is I'm building may not resemble the finished picture but I'll have made it myself, it will be sturdy and should last long enough and, most importantly, I can dismantle it and rebuild it as and when I feel like it. Because right now, rebuilding seems to be what's needed. My foundations are rotten and, because of that, all the things I've layered on top of them aren't functioning right and are collapsing. I may end up paying a steep price for ignoring the books, hospitals, doctors and various gurus who take the money and leave the wreckage for me to deal with, but it's got to be cheaper than carrying on like this.

I am a 7-year-old trapped in a 41-year-old's body, so it's going to be tough but I just can't go on like this any more. No more asking my shrink for solutions or following a bunch of confusing rules set by other people, real or imagined. Just me finding my own way, wrong turns and all. I'm going to look like a dick at times, I'm going to say the wrong things and act like an idiot, but I do that already and I'd rather do it authentically, as the real me. I've got to believe that, occasionally, I'm going to start to get things right a bit more often.

I promise myself that when I do get things right I'm going to remember it, learn from it, repeat it and embrace it. Because that means that I have a shot at really, truly enjoying my career, my life, my weird little world. I could be able to function well enough in relationships, sustain friendships and be a better father. And I could go to sleep feeling content, unashamed, worthy and in integrity with myself. Rather than feeling like a fraud who is simply killing time while the world collapses around me.

And so it starts. I wake up one morning and put on my 'not giving a fuck' coat, like a mischievous Harry Potter character donning his invisibility cloak. I start thinking about the record label meeting I didn't dare cancel when I went through my diary, and decide to rearrange it after all. I spend the next twenty-seven hours watching TV, cleaning the flat, walking, napping, tinkling about on the piano. It was the right thing to do. Fucks given? Zero.

Moments of loneliness come and go. I avoid the tendency to try to fix the moments when I feel isolated. I just sit with the difficult feelings and wait for them to pass, and sure enough they do. Clouds in the sky.

Physically I get even sicker. Coughing, sneezing, a fever. As a result, I'm losing huge chunks of time, something that happens regularly enough anyway – even when I'm healthy – to not be too disturbing. I've always dissociated, and it used to be much worse, but it's creeping back a little more regularly, especially with so little sleep. The clock will move magically from 10 a.m. to 3 p.m. and I'll have no clue what has happened in between. As ever when this happens, my body is there but my soul is somewhere else entirely. It's why the piano is so good for me. Time can disappear but I know I'm safe because playing the piano allows the imaginative part of my mind to dominate the anxious part and take over, even if only for a brief hour or two. When that happens, I'm automatically disconnected from difficult feelings and connected to something without words or danger. I spend a lot of time during this strange week or two shuffling to my piano to practise.

And anyway I don't worry too much about missing hours. Days I'd worry about. An afternoon, not so much.

I head up to Bristol for a concert at St George's which is one of my favourite venues. I'm feeling under the weather and there's a journalist from *Der Spiegel* with me, interviewing me on the train, but she's very gentle and I don't mind. I'm working on not giving a fuck about the concert, in a good way. Knowing people have paid to come see me, respecting both that and the composers' intentions but at the same time not worrying about what might happen, not overthinking it, trusting that I've got this. A few weeks previously my lovely shrink had said to me that being in front of the piano is the one place I resolutely *didn't* need to worry and where I could absolutely trust that I know what I'm doing. Every other area of my life is no doubt a different story, but the piano is my safe place, my musical panic room. In fact, I'm kind of looking forward to being in front of those eighty-eight keys and being able to disappear in plain sight for an hour and a half. It's a bit like a mental holiday, and God knows I need one of those.

It goes really well. I'm happy with how I play. I demolish a giant burger afterwards with the journalist and go to bed happy. I don't care that it's pissing down with rain, that I've got a cold and have to get up at 8 a.m. to catch a train to Cheltenham. I'm just there, quietly not giving a fuck about the trivial stuff, lying in bed, reading, lights off, drifting into sleep, figuring I'll get a few hours and it'll be good enough because it has to be.

Which is what happens. I seem to have more energy inside me to direct at the important things and I feel so much more optimistic about life. It's not just the reallocation of emotional resources that's helping – it is dawning on me more and more that despite the brutal cost of the 'parking ticket', the amount of energy freed up has been unbelievable. After an eye-opening event at Cheltenham's medical charity festival, Medicine Unboxed, where doctors and scientists (and me) discuss how medicine can be more creative than just being about meds, I'm driven home to London and jump straight into bed. I'm exhausted to the point that my face is twitching again and I can't really think straight (as if I ever could anyway). I get up for a lazy curry delivery and get right back into bed, thinking that actually this could be a pretty awesome way to spend a few days. During the night I have vivid dreams. Violent and scary ones. My eyes ping open, terrified, at 3.38 a.m., wide awake. But instead of panicking I make a cup of tea and sit quietly, leaning into the fear and the loneliness, and my heart rate starts to lower and my head starts to calm down and cool down, and I fall back asleep around six for a couple of hours.

I spend three days sick in bed, feeling like death, my body letting go of and expelling what feels like years of toxicity, and holding on to the fact that I have only two more concerts to do. I remind myself that I have two weeks off for myself during the Christmas break. Until then I can hold it together. My mind and my body are doing their best to hold firm but it's difficult; I can feel things threatening to crumble despite my best intentions. Losing time, middle-of-the-night fevers, little sleep, forgetfulness, chatting to myself out loud, little OCD tics and tocs coming and going. I even cut my cigarette intake down to seven a day to try and help my adrenal system a bit. But I'm still holding firm to this new sense of freedom and calm. Being sick is frustrating. But it is what it is. Fighting myself and chastising myself isn't going to help anything. And that sense of freedom is deeper and somehow resides far beneath the surface stuff of illness and day-to-day worries.

It's soon time to get back to work. I hunker down for a few more precious hours, resting as much as possible, then I pack my bags, breathe deep and remind myself that all of these performances will serve me well when it comes to the recording. I've usually done it the other way round – record pieces and then perform them live. But this time I've really got to know these works. I've crawled around inside them with the lights off and examined every nook and cranny, I've lived and breathed them for months, and by the time I get to the studio in Aldeburgh, they will be as fully known to me as they could ever be. In a way, these concerts are a rehearsal for a recording which can never be deleted, and I need to make sure it's going to be worthy of that.

The two last concerts are in – you guessed it – Spain. Valencia and then Zaragoza.

Three good things happen in Valencia.

1. I don't give in to the pressure of feeling totally inadequate and like a fraud. There is a national TV crew filming the rehearsal and some photographers taking snaps as I prepare for the gig on stage. One of them has been photographing only classical musicians, mainly pianists, for twenty-five years. She tells me that she's recently photographed both Grigory Sokolov and Arcadi Volodos (TTH™s the pair of them; in fact, the two greatest pianists I can think of who are still living). They'd both been photographed on the same stage I'm currently sitting on. Which blows my fucking mind wide open. Here I am again, sharing the same stage as the greats, and my gut reaction is to feel a shabby fraction of a man in comparison. But what's good is that this time the voice of optimism is louder than the self-hate one.

   Because if I'd been playing the piano religiously since the age of three and been brought up in Russia I'd no doubt be every inch their equal. But I haven't. I'm from north London, had no formal training until I was fourteen and I stopped playing completely for a decade from the age of eighteen. Of course I'm not going to be their equal. Idiot. Just as they can do things I can't do, I'm doing something they couldn't do either. So I let it go after the initial stab of self-doubt, and just giggle at the fact that somehow I've ended up on the same stage and playing the same piano as these guys. It's amusing now, like a really cool dream that's come true, rather than a reason to aggressively self-harm.

2. I actually welcome Denis's micro-managing. I see it for what it is: he is being helpful to try and make me perform better. Twenty minutes before the show he's giving me phrases in Spanish and asking me to drop them into the show. He takes his seat and, as I'm in the wings waiting to go on, he starts texting the promoter asking her to tell me other things to do and say on stage. This would have felt like total overwhelm before: here I am trying to hold tens of thousands of notes in my head, ready to perform them from memory, each note ascribed a very specific finger and each phrase honed over and prac-tised for countless hours, pedal and weight of arms and breathing and phrasing and tone all worked on. Added to that I have to remember dates, anecdotes, the arc of the story I'm going to be telling everyone in between playing these pieces. Receiving new instructions, especially in a different language, which I have to try and shoehorn into all of that used to spin me out. It's still stressful, but I don't fall apart.

3. The big one: I fuck up on stage but I don't let it unsettle me. I decided at the last minute to switch my first two pieces around – the *Polonaise-fantasie* first and then the F minor *Fantasie*. It felt like perhaps that was a better way to do it, given the structure of the fantasy narrative I talk about during the show. Because of the change in order, I have a small memory lapse while I play the *Polonaise-fan-tasie*. It's my first memory lapse of the entire tour. It's only

two bars, and unless you know the piece really well you wouldn't ever have realised – there's no hesitation, no pause, no gap in the flow. But *I* know. And it's something else to club me over the head with, if the *Reservoir Dogs* team choose to do so. But here's the thing: as I play, a voice comes into my head telling me this is my penultimate show of the year, I'm worth more than this, I can enjoy it and get on with it and relish the fact that I'm here in the exact same spot Sokolov has been, and if someone had told me, even five years ago, let alone twenty-five years ago, that this would be happening I'd have shat my pants with glee. I push on through, and it's all fine.

As we approach Zaragoza, I realise I really am experiencing something new. I realise I'm finally getting this unshakeable feeling that after all the torture and shit, although my internal life isn't perfect, self-help book friendly, filled with affirmations of the best kind, and can't just be about Beethoven and Bach and Chopin, it's actually something special and worthy and noble. It's an imperfect life for sure, but, just possibly, it's a good enough life despite those imperfections.

In fact, good things happen in Zaragoza too. It's my last gig of the tour and I want to give it all I've got. Which I do. Everything comes off – no memory issues, my fingers feel solid, my head blissfully quiet. The audience is amazing. Absolute concentration. I give five encores including, for the first time, that amazing Puccini transcription – I'd only picked it up a few weeks previously and it's feeling more and more solid. And, with the sound and the acoustic of this enormous aircraft hangar of a venue, the notes just seem to hang there like magic. It feels great and, despite cold season being in full swing, there's total silence from the audience. Also, I manage to watch the last half of the Abu Dhabi Grand Prix on my phone backstage. Which makes me super happy, even if Lewis lost the championship to Rosberg. It's still my favourite sport in the world – any sport where if you blink in the wrong place or lose concentration for a split second you could end up going into a cement wall at 200mph has got to be worth respecting.

I'm walking back from the venue and I realise that it's all over. These past few weeks of relentless touring and travel and madness is done and put to bed, and I allow myself a little spring in my step and a smile to spread across my face.

When I get back to the hotel I notice my Twitter feed go nuts because *Salvados*, that Sunday night Spanish TV show, has just shown the trailer for my episode which will air the following week. Everyone seems very excited about it. I'm terrified because I've not seen it; I just remember how excruciatingly embarrassed I felt about my playing, and I know I overshared during the interviews. But it's out of my hands. My hope, my only real hope, is that perhaps it will help continue what has only recently started in Spain when it comes to talking about child abuse, something that has become an epidemic and a taboo one to boot. It will, just maybe, help to lessen the shame, collective and otherwise.

It turns out, of course, that I needn't have worried. A week later the show airs and it's handled delicately, respectfully, and in the right way. The producers have made a film I'm immensely proud to have been a part of. I don't see a single negative comment on social media (because I'm still shallow enough to want to pay attention to things like that) and, again, feel just a little bit happy that the show shone a very bright light on an issue so close to my heart.

I feel a bit all over the place as I prepare to leave Zaragoza. I hope there won't be some kind of crash and comedown now. But I also know that if there is, I've got some time and space to allow that to happen. Most importantly, I feel that maybe now I may be in a place where I can handle it safely and gently.

I've learned something these last few weeks through bitter experience that no self-help book could possibly have achieved for me. I've really, truly learned that despite what my head tells me, it is, the vast majority of the time, completely wrong and acting on false information. I've played dozens of gigs in dozens of cities in a few short weeks and they were all great, really. I've travelled alone without Denis and played gigs in challenging venues perfectly well. I've played when I was sick and exhausted and have done fine – even in Vienna when everything turned to shit. I've played broken-hearted and while dealing with major life upsets and nobody could tell. I've managed to wrestle my head into submission and focus on the bigger picture, the music, the important stuff. I've realised that concerts aren't life or death, that there are a million things I can't control and that none of them really matter. I've realised that even if I haven't lined all my things up immaculately in my dressing-room table before a show and I discover that two of them are touching each other when I get back after the concert, nothing bad has happened or will happen. That I can do last-minute press and interviews, and learn phrases in a foreign language just before a concert. I can handle delayed flights and going without smoking for a few hours.

I have an unusual feeling inside me. I think it's a small amount of pride in myself.

The next morning, after broken sleep and peculiar dreams, I wake up tired but satisfied, jump in a cab, catch the train to Madrid, a taxi to the airport, a plane to London, a train to Paddington, the tube to home, and shut the door on everything but piano and pals and rest for a couple of weeks. I've got a recording to prepare for. It's my most important one so far. But this time I'm ready for it not to be the tortuous mind-fuck other gigs and recordings have been. It's time to take a breath and start to move forward as I mean to go on – hopeful, content and with the expectation of good things. Because a growing part of me is starting to believe that that is not only possible but even, dare I say it, deserved.

AFFIRMATION 8:

'Everything is going to be OK
in the end. If it's not OK,
then it's not the end.'

TRANSLATION:

'THERE'S A CHANCE (A BIGGER ONE THAN YOU THINK)
THAT ALL WILL BE WELL.'

Rachmaninov Étude-Tableau Op. 39/5

Sergei Rachmaninov's unapologetic emotionalism is what endears him the most to me. In 1917, the year of the Russian Revolution, with Sergei himself in enforced exile, he completed a set of piano studies that perfectly mirror the dark and clouded love he had for his country of birth. They are short stories, inspired by paintings the source of which he never revealed, but expressing the deepest of deep Russian feelings. There is no joy, no hope, no humour. A hard-won sense of triumph right at the end of the last one is the most uplifted we get. Like most of his music, they are transcendentally difficult to play. Sergei had the most enormous hands and could span twelve piano keys with one hand, making it catastrophically challenging for us normally endowed pianists. The great pianist Gary Graffman once lamented the fact that he hadn't learned more of Rachmaninov's works when he was a teenager and 'too young to know fear'.

The fifth one of the set of nine is the best known and, for me, the most emotionally bleak. Its coarse textures layer voice upon voice, three or four different melodies at once sometimes, as it produces climax after climax of shattering emotional intensity.

It carries on where Chopin and Liszt left off with their études in the pursuit of technical progression, and even expands on it. Like Chopin, Liszt and Debussy, Rachmaninov is one of the few composers who manages to turn working on technical issues into pure art. This is a piece filled with the biggest of feelings, and ones which leave the listener, and the performer, wiser and better for having experienced them.

Best of all, it permits, even encourages, the pianist to beat seven shades of shit out of the piano. It's a group therapy session where we begin by eavesdropping and by the end we have joined in and shared something profoundly personal. After much noisy tragedy, the piece dies away and ends quietly, spent, in the major key. He's gone through his hero's journey, fought the good fight and emerged the other side battered and bruised but still alive and, I like to think, even more resilient.

*

ALDEBURGH, DECEMBER 2016

I drive down to Aldeburgh for the recording, the culmination of this tour, my way of putting down on disc the music that has sustained me, captivated me, inspired me and kept me afloat during the mad periods. It's a big, big deal for me. The sun is shining, everything feels crisp, hopeful and fresh.

After hurtling down the A12, I find Snape Maltings buzzing with pre-Christmas shoppers of a certain age. It's a beautiful part of the world. I let myself into the most perfect little cottage, right by the studio, and dump my scores and bag. I have a moment where I wish I could share this with someone. The cottage. Suffolk. Steinways. Recording. Neumann microphones. I want to talk for hours about it and have someone here with me to get excited too. But I don't allow myself to dwell on this. Instead, I go find a café where I sit alone and demolish a proper Christmas roast turkey lunch. I buy snacks (chocolate for energy and perhaps comfort, milk and cereal for breakfast) and go back to the cottage to study my scores.

I'm getting good at disaster prevention. Rather than hide out alone and overthink, I put my own version of crisis management in place and arrange to meet Andrew the producer for dinner.

Andrew Keener.

One of the best classical music producers in the world, a cross between Sir George Martin and Rick Rubin, but for my kind of music.

This is so significant to me. So, literally, vital. Ever since I was a kid I've seen Andrew's name on the CDs of all of my heroes with a producing credit. I didn't know what a producer did back then but he was clearly an integral part of the process. About twelve or thirteen years ago when I quit my job in the City I thought perhaps I could be a producer myself, given that there was no way I'd be able to become a concert pianist.

A producer basically sits in the booth in the recording studio, music scores in front of him, and listens to the musician playing. Anything that sounds wrong, could be better, is slightly off centre, a little bit wonky or runs counter to what feels right or what the composer has indicated, is marked down with a combination of coloured pencils. He or she then, tactfully, lets the musician know and another take is recorded. This goes on and on until both producer and musician feel they have everything covered, have a mutually agreed-upon interpretation and got rid of any fluffed notes. Then the producer works his or her ass off editing and, ahem, producing, the finished album. They patch all the best takes together (anything from 100 to 1,000 of them) have the sound engineer master it (make it sound amazing), and send through the first edit to the musician.

Who then wants to die, sends through about a thousand notes and requests for changes, improvements and re-edits, and a weird, hyper-sensitive back and forth goes on for a few weeks until, finally, there is a version of the album everyone is happy (enough) with. It's a bit like what an editor does with a writer.

Producers in effect play God. They need to hear one bum note in a rush of ten thousand, isolate it, let the pianist know it was a bum note (politely), make sure there's enough good material to complete the album and always let the pianist think that, as soloist, they are in charge. While knowing full well that without a good producer they'd be royally fucked.

Anyway. So many years ago I wanted to be a producer. Because I figured I'd spend my life in recording studios with my idols listening to music all day and that was a pretty cool second best to being an actual pianist. So I email this uber-producer Andrew Keener and manage to wangle a meeting. We meet at a session he's doing and it's a bit weird. He doesn't seem to take me that seriously and is kind of distracted. Nothing comes of it. I'm irritated and quite upset but kind of expected it – I had no background or training in music production and was working in the City at the time, just another corporate asshole.

Eventually I end up becoming a pianist anyway (full details and more info available in *Instrumental*, which is for sale in all good book stores. And Amazon). But then, early 2016, I get a handwritten letter (remember those?) out of the blue. It's from Andrew Keener. He says I'm sure I won't remember him but we met a few years ago and he was a bit of a dick to me and thought I was a bit of a waste of time. But that he'd recently read my book (*Instrumental*, still on sale, still paying off the legal bills incurred in getting it published) and having read it he feels 'deeply ashamed' of how he treated me and if he could ever do anything to put it right I only had to ask.

Of course I call him because, well what a lovely fucking letter and also, Andrew Keener! The only guy in the world I can talk in forensic detail with about recording sessions with the greatest pianists who ever lived. I get hold of him and tell him I hadn't thought about it at all (lie) and certainly had no hard feelings (double lie) and ask him about four hundred questions about all my hero pianist idols: Evgeny Kissin, Stephen Hough, Marc-André Hamelin, Arcadi Volodos, Andrei Gavrilov, Vladimir Horowitz, Martha Argerich, Annie Fischer, Jorge Bolet, Olli Mustonen, Mikhail Pletnev, Sviatoslav Richter, Emil Gilels, Krystian Zimerman, Murray Perahia, Ivo Pogorelich, Denis Matsuev, Anatol Ugorski etc. etc. etc. And when I've calmed down (eighty-seven minutes and change) he says to me he's got my recordings and loves them, and if I ever wanted him to produce my next one he'd be honoured.

How. About. Them. Apples.

I think about it for a microsecond while my head catches up with my 'holy shit moment' and then shriek 'YES, PLEASE'.

All of which is a long-winded way of saying that recording this album of late Beethoven, Chopin, Rachmaninov etc. is going to be extra special for me because Keener will be producing it.

The two of us wander down to the local pub with Mike, the uber-sound guy. My own particular kind of Christmas has come early because for two whole hours we chat incessantly about pianists, music, composers, recordings, conductors, piano concertos, recording venues, pianos, producers, managers, record labels, individual bars in individual recordings of random pieces, individual notes in individual bars in individual recordings of random pieces . . . All the things I can't talk about with anyone else because it's so delightfully niche. It is without a doubt the best dinner I've had in months. Anecdotes about Barenboim, Kissin, Hough, Pletnev and others, all of whom Andrew has produced. I am in my element. Properly geeking out about the most ridiculous things because they feel the same way as me about all this stuff, albeit turned down a fraction. I am filled to the brim with joy. A kid at the big boys' table. I don't even notice that I've been sitting down in a restaurant all this time.

I tell them I've set a target of recording thirty-five minutes of music tomorrow, which they agree seems doable if slightly ambitious. I want to start with Op. 110 and then do the *Polonaise-fantasie*, and figure if I can nail those in one day I'm going to be flying and filled with confidence by the end of day one. They are the loveliest couple of guys and it all feels so magical, so easy. It's one of those rare moments for me when I am so relaxed with the company I'm in that I drop the mask(s) and am completely myself, all childish enthusiasm and adult focus. Which for music, for anything creative, is the best possible combination.

Two and a half hours in a restaurant. And I don't even want to get laid. This is what music does for me.

I get back to my cottage and fall into bed dreaming about tomorrow. About finally having everything converge on this one place and point in time – these composers, this venue, this producer, these pieces, all of which I've admired beyond compare since I was a kid. Here I am and it's about to happen.

I realise my outlook has been getting more and more positive since I began doing things to move towards the pain, not away from it. It started gradually, and with the tour and its huge ups and downs, it's slowly gathered momentum. It looks like we have such an aversion to pain that our gut does all it can to avoid it, but the truth is I think it's only by going towards it, almost making friends with it, that we can find some kind of peace and acceptance. It reminds me of that story about Second World War pilots who, when their planes went into a spin, would do all they could to pull their planes up and out of it and back up into the air, and yet they kept crashing and dying. It was only when they started to move *into* the dive that they realised this was the way out – down, through and towards almost certain death before their engines would restart and they'd end up turning full circle, back in the air flying steady.

If none of the difficult things had happened to me when I was younger, I don't think I'd be here in this place. And it seems to me that, really, truly, it doesn't matter that I'm alone. It doesn't matter that I am at times terrified of myself and my feelings. It doesn't matter that I am awkward and messy and imperfect and a bit weird. Because just for this moment everything has been worth it simply to be here, to breathe in the sea air, to hear Beethoven's immortal music in my head and heart and know that tomorrow I'm going to be pushing it out through my hands and preparing to send it out into the atmosphere for anyone who wants to listen. I decide here and now to dedicate it quietly to the six-year-old me who had to (literally) suck up all that pain and deal with the hell of my toxic fucking childhood in order that he can be here now – fit, thrilled and, hopefully, able to do justice to the thing that has sustained him for all these years.

I wake up at 5 a.m. Too excited. Filled with nerves, expectation and adrenalin, music flooding my brain. We'd arranged to meet and start recording at 10 a.m. Predictably I get to the studio at 8 a.m., and of course it's closed. I come back every ten minutes, desperate to get in and try the piano. At 8.40 the tuner is there and I'm allowed in. The studio is enormous, with a huge, oak vaulted ceiling and the biggest windows I've ever seen (I wish I could shove a photo in here – stalk me on Instagram/Twitter instead and you'll see what I mean). The stone walls are irregularly curved to help with the acoustics. Mike is there too, setting up his microphones – an art form in and of itself. At 9.30 I jump on the piano and warm up. It's perfect. Andrew is there with his scores and by 10 a.m. we're ready to go.

I want to settle in before tackling the Beethoven so I decide to record one of two Chopin nocturnes that I want on this album. Without them the album would only be sixty minutes or so, which feels a bit cheap. And an extra fourteen minutes of Chopin is always a good thing. They are perfectly suited to a fantasy-based album, composed to fill the hinterland between waking and sleep, dreams and reality. Middle-of-the-night music to keep us company and send our demons to bed. The B major one I've chosen to record first is almost impressionistic in its harmonies, its soundscape is ethereal as fuck and on that piano in that room it sounds magnificent. It's eight minutes long and packed with intense inner beauty and fragility. There's an extended passage near the end filled with trills that so often trips pianists up – to maintain such rapid movement for so long, especially at a low volume, is fantastically difficult. It takes me a few takes to get it as good as I feel I can but I think we get there in the end. It's a trust issue – Andrew tells me we have it and I've got to believe him and let it go and move on. Which is so fucking hard. I could spend the entire day on these eight bars. But I'm terrified we'll run out of time. I go with it and accept he has no reason to lie to me.

We move onto the Beethoven.

I do one entire take of the whole thing and then we go movement by movement. I'm happy with 80 per cent of the first couple of takes and then we really get into the detail as we narrow down the length of new takes and focus on specific areas and bars. Doing it all in the same session means it doesn't lose its sense of structure and I don't drop concentration or forget the speeds I've chosen. It takes us some time, especially that nightmare second movement psycho passage of flying hands and crazy fast notes. But we get there and I'm confident it's OK. Perhaps even good in places. I can't stop myself playing and working. Andrew keeps telling me I'm a 'workhorse' and to try and relax a bit. But I can't. I have to get this done and out of me and put to bed.

We've hit twenty-nine minutes by 3.30 p.m. I haven't played this much and with this much focus for a long time. My wrists are sore, my arms tight, my shoulders complaining. Which makes it sound perhaps more heroic than it actually is. But piano playing is physical and I'm not the biggest guy in the world. Nevertheless, I want to push through with the *Polonaise-fantasie*. I do two full takes and then break it down. There are some challenging moments. I feel as if I'm losing heart, that Andrew is tolerating me, indulging me rather than treating me as a proper musician. But I'm aware that may just be my head and that's because I'm tired. Up since five, working intensely, weary, emotional, cranky. I've learned not to trust my mind when I'm like this.

We reach the coda (which has some bastard-challenging passagework) and I decide to call it quits for the night. I've reached my limit.

By now I feel hyper-needy and a bit all over the place. I didn't really expect this, but I'm not surprised. I guess I thought we'd nail everything quickly and confidently and I wouldn't doubt or question things. Which is idiotic because it's me we're talking about, and of course I'm going to feel fragile about it. I've also spent eight or nine hours playing at full pelt with little sleep and even less conversation. It's the musical equivalent of cabin fever.

I walk out of the studio, and instead of letting the voices take over, I sit quietly for a bit, talking myself down. I've recorded forty-one minutes today. Andrew and Mike are both happy. Tomorrow I'll finish up the *Polonaise* and hopefully most of the other pieces, leaving Wednesday free to cover anything left over or any sections we fancy doing again. I also have to leave Aldeburgh earlier than I thought on Wednesday because getting a visa for my upcoming US gigs is proving harder than getting an audience with the pope and I need to get new passport photos done and forms filled out and witnessed before I fly to Madrid on Thursday. Focus on the practicalities, don't let the mind unravel. Rinse and repeat.

I still feel stressed, and find a tree to sit and smoke under. I try and convince myself that it's just the first day and to chill the fuck out. Tomorrow I'll be fresher and more confident knowing I've broken the back of it. Again, I remind myself to trust Andrew. Knowing that if he wasn't satisfied with my playing, then he wouldn't allow me to move on until it was sounding right. After all, his name is going to be on this album too. Fuck, I hate not being able to control everything, but I can't hear what he hears and I need to accept he's been doing this for forty years and knows his shit. I finish my smoke and walk back into his booth to ask him outright if it's going to be OK and if he has enough good material. He is adamant it will be and that he does. He reassures me he'll re-listen to things tomorrow and if there's anything he's unsure of we will revisit them. I feel slightly better. The fish and chips at dinner help too.

I get to bed and collapse, praying I'll sleep past 5 a.m. and that my muscles will rest and recharge overnight. Tomorrow is more Chopin and some Rachmaninov and I want to be ready.

*

257

I needn't have worried (once again that same goddam refrain). I slept like someone with nothing on their conscience, woke up energised and focused. Started working at 9 a.m., and by 4.30 p.m. I'd reached sixty-eight minutes of music recorded and in the can. Which is amazing. Andrew tells me he's not really collaborated with someone who works quite so intensely and without breaks (other than the occasional five-minute smoke). Not sure if it's a compliment, but I'll take it.

Chopin's F minor *Fantasie* is the big piece today. It feels comfortable, solid and secure. Next comes another epic Chopin nocturne, this time the big C minor one, one of his greatest compositions and in effect a tone poem, operatic and huge, filled with longing, simmering rage, grief, desolation and, of course, love. Unusually for Chopin there are some really insane double octaves, Liszt-style in this piece – both hands stretched really wide and hammering rapidly up and down the keyboard at the same time. And the contrast between that virtuosic cacophony and the quiet, quasi-religious chorale that precedes it only adds to the sense of fantasy and insanity. Then Rachmaninov's monumental last prelude with those ridiculously huge fistfuls of notes that had been such fun to play during the tour.

Needing to calm down after that (all the octaves and giant chords making me sweat like a smuggler going through Bangkok airport) I play the short, soft Puccini transcription. Everything is coming much more easily today than yesterday. There are isolated moments of doubt and worry but Andrew talks me down and encourages me. In his super-sweet way, he lets me know if something isn't quite right ever so thoughtfully ('I wonder if perhaps you'd like to try that one more time just to make an old man like me happy', 'I'm sure it's the piano, but could you try and coax a slightly warmer sound out of those four bars?' etc.) and between the two of us, along with Mike's considerable expertise in sound, I think we might be making a decent record.

Towards the end of the session I am working on the last piece, the Rachmaninov Étude Tableau. It's bleak. All Russian and vodka, angst and persecution and long walks through the Siberian tundra. It's also the musical equivalent of bodybuilding.

And I break the piano. One of the hammers snaps and one of the strings has gone properly wonky.

I blame Rachmaninov.

The technician has to be called and it is going to take a while to fix. I do the unthinkable and say I am going to leave it for the day and come back to it tomorrow. Because I'm well ahead of schedule and, much more importantly, Andrew and I are working and flowing and doing everything just right. Also because, well, I'm a different person now, kind of. I don't need to force things out of fear any more. I know it's the right decision. I feel about three stone lighter as I wander back to my cottage to catch up on emails, shower and spend some quiet time alone. My forearms and wrists are tight and sore, but there's no sharp pain, so nothing to really worry about. My head is calm.

Andrew is getting to know me well now. He suggests I might prefer to have dinner alone tonight while he listens to everything we've done so far so that tomorrow we can focus on anything we might have missed. Which is exactly what I want. Early dinner with a book and then an early night so I can finish off the Rachmaninov and any extras in the morning.

As I lie in the dark I allow myself to check in with my emotions. It seems to me that rather than have them hijack me when things get too much, it's better to pre-empt things and make a conscious effort to see what's going on in my head at semi-regular intervals before they escalate. I am cautiously optimistic. I'm exhausted in a good way. And I'm happy. Content. I don't think I've let anyone down, living or dead, and there were definitely moments in that studio where I felt as if I played as well as I could have.

The end of this year is so close I can taste it. This record, somehow the culmination of so much more than a calendar year, is almost put to bed and it's nearly time to let it go and surrender. Easy in principle, and yet something I've always struggled with. Perhaps now, for the first time, I can rest easy knowing I've done my best, given it everything I've got and start looking ahead with a smile rather than always looking over my shoulder with suspicion, regret and doubt. That way my bastard head won't win.

I fall asleep, drunk on music, enthusiasm and countryside, and wake up for the final few hours of recording. Andrew, true to his word, has gone over everything and has four small queries – tiny things that are probably noticeable only to him and me, but I'm glad he's found them and we redo them until we're happy.

We spend another hour finishing up the immense Rachmaninov étude. I genuinely feel on my last legs by this point. This piece is filled with such monstrous chords, so many fortissimo octaves and leaps and runs that it requires immense energy. I push as hard as I can and give it all I've got because I know this is my last chance.

Suddenly – unexpectedly, even – we're done. The final take is in the bag, the crew seem satisfied and it's all over.

There are hugs and goodbyes and then I'm haring back to London in my car to sort visas and admin stuff. All I'm doing as I'm driving home is running through everything we've just recorded in my head, looking for things I could've done better. Which is idiotic because (a) it's too late and (b) my memory is nowhere near good enough to do that accurately. So I tell myself to stop it and I spend the final ninety minutes of my drive practising letting go.

Letting go.

The end result of the last few months has been the realisation that no matter what is going on in my outer world, it is only by accepting things at a core level and giving up my incessant, pathological need to control, protect, defend and secure myself that I have a shot of finding any real, lasting happiness. If I can't do that then I'm back to simply existing. Existing while dying by millimetres. I've had enough of that way of life. Like many of us, I feel like a freak too much of the time as it is. These last five months have been both brutal and liberating and they have reaffirmed that letting go of the things that cause me pain is a lifelong pursuit. Peace is not going to come from castigating myself when things go even slightly wrong, treating myself like shit, relying on psychologically flawed mechanisms that functioned thirty-five years ago as an emergency ripcord but were never meant to be sustainable long term. Peace will come only from self-awareness, from surrendering to the siege in my head rather than constantly defending against it.

There is nothing wrong with the fact that there is an onslaught of nastiness in my mind that sometimes gets unleashed without warning and at a moment's notice. There can't be anything wrong with that; it is the human condition in all its ugly magnificence. Making friends with that, learning to quieten it by gently accepting things and no longer fighting them, shifting the focus onto other more gentle areas – this is my way out of the war zone I've been inhabiting for so long. I feel like I've been battling against fear for the longest time, and perhaps now I really understand that in today's reality there *is* no battle. If there ever was, then I lost. And I lost happily. Because that means it's over and I don't need to fight any more.

Konrad Lorenz said that the human soul is very much older than the human mind. What a comforting thought. The soul is also much gentler than the mind. More whole. Wiser. I've lost count of the times I should have been either arrested or sectioned for having too much to think. My thoughts are more often than not dirty, class A drugs, and the awful irony is that the dealer is no one other than myself. My best thinking has got me curled up in a ball in psych wards, alone and terrified.

Since I was a kid I have instructed my mind to do an impossible job in the belief that should it fail in this job then I will die. I have directed it, repeatedly and consistently, to constantly analyse, solve, fix, guard, figure out, manipulate, examine, predict, determine, protect, understand, compartmentalise, make sense of and explain every single facet of my life, real or imagined, twenty-four hours a day. All of this so I can enjoy the dubious illusion of feeling safe. Over time it has simply buckled under the pressure. How could it not? The pressure of having to maintain that level of mental activity, combined with such an impossible goal and an overworked, stressed-out psyche has left me exhausted, paranoid, broken and terrified of far too many things. It turns out I have given all my fucks away to things that didn't even deserve them in the first place.

Exposure to sustained trauma oftentimes forces the brain to rewire itself, especially in childhood when it is still malleable. And during that process, my mind's wires became all tangled up. The headphone cables from hell. Made of barbed wire and now fused and condensed into a thick, impenetrable ball of steel. Injunctions, legal battles and a marital breakdown have only compounded things further.

Simply put, I do not know how to live well and I do not know how to live effectively.

If that is ever to change then I fear it is going to take many more years and a lot more practice than my piano playing has ever received. And this year I have started, ever so slowly, to untangle things, especially in the weeks since my trip to Vienna. I've had moments on tour or back at my little London flat, of dropping my negative thoughts and allowing the stillness that exists underneath to sneak to the fore and work its magic. And those moments have been the best ones of the year. It's happened mostly on stage, mid-performance, but on occasion I've found a way to bring that into my everyday life. The relief has been immediate and profound. The siege interrupted, the ambush over, the peace overwhelming.

I know I am not alone in feeling like this, of being in desperate need of untangling and learning how to let go. I can't quite bring myself to believe that I am one of the tiny few who is constantly fucking things up while everyone else is quite happily living their lives with no ups and downs, doubts and worries, and middle-of-the-night freak-outs.

If I'm right, if we *are* all varying degrees of fucked up, and the twenty-first century's human condition has morphed from the past's very real terror of getting eaten by giant mammoths, attacked by roaming tribes of Neanderthals and starving or freezing to death, into the illusory yet similarly intense anxiety of work deadlines, iPhone battery life and social conformity, then we all need to figure out how to change our fucking priorities. And quickly too, because life expectancy is already short enough.

Life being what it is, no doubt there will always be fire on all sides. But maybe, just maybe, it could be a less intense heat. A lovely, crackling living-room hearth rather than an all-consuming forest blaze. Living in the middle of that fire could just be pleasantly warm and occasionally rather fun, not a feeling of being trapped in a terrifying inferno with no way out, just waiting to be burned alive.

Remember those scenes at the end of *Così fan tutte* and *Figaro* when they all get together and sing their hearts out, forgiving each other and celebrating that love is perfectly flawed? It's incredible that I've listened to those operas so many times, and it's only now that I really get it. That to truly love both self and others means you have to accept the agony as well as the ecstasy that comes with it, and that is what makes love so real, special and worthwhile. Same goes for life.

The immortal Miles Davis said about music that 'anybody can play. The note is only 20 percent. The attitude of the motherfucker who plays it is 80 percent.' Again, same goes for life. Anybody can live, survive, physically exist. Getting through each day is only 20 per cent. But living *well*, loving and laughing, learning and growing, creating and enjoying, that remaining, magnificent 80 per cent, is entirely down to our motherfucking attitude.

Life is messy and imperfect, and yet it also has a fragility and humanity to it that is beautiful, gentle and profoundly soothing. Like music, this fragility can unite us all in the most comforting way. After creating so much unnecessary pain and hurt for myself, being so desperate to appear better and more normal than I actually am in every area of my life, filling my days and nights with self-doubt, worry, nausea-inducing anxiety and visceral self-hatred, I'll tell you one thing I've never been more sure of: I'm not going to disregard that 80 per cent any longer. It's time to stop fighting and to start accepting, even celebrating the things I've been ashamed of for so long – the awkward moments, the clumsy mistakes, the fuck-ups, slip-ups and errors, the simple, honest mortality of my own existence. It's time to stop merely surviving and start actually *living*; authentically and with a bit of compassion both for myself and for the little boy I once was who was so savagely hurt. Because living like this is the *only* effective way to put out the fire that surrounds me and set myself free.

I return home to my little flat. It's nearly Christmas. My son is arriving soon. And I'm OK.